The Reference Shelf®

New Media

Edited by Albert Rolls

The Reference Shelf
Volume 78 • Number 2

The H. W. Wilson Company
2006

The Reference Shelf

The books in this series contain reprints of articles, excerpts from books, addresses on current issues, and studies of social trends in the United States and other countries. There are six separately bound numbers in each volume, all of which are usually published in the same calendar year. Numbers one through five are each devoted to a single subject, providing background information and discussion from various points of view and concluding with a subject index and comprehensive bibliography that lists books, pamphlets, and abstracts of additional articles on the subject. The final number of each volume is a collection of recent speeches, and it contains a cumulative speaker index. Books in the series may be purchased individually or on subscription.

Library of Congress has cataloged this title as follows:

New media / edited by Albert Rolls.
        p. cm.—(The Reference shelf; v. 78, no. 2)
  Includes bibliographical references and index.
  ISBN 0-8242-1060-3 (alk. paper)
  1. Multimedia systems. 2. Multimedia systems—Social aspects. 3. Digital media.
4. Digital media—Social aspects. I. Rolls, Albert. II. Series.
    QA76.575.N477 2006
    006.7—dc22

                                              2006001403

Cover: A South Korean man uses wireless Internet at a coffee shop in 2005 in Seoul, South Korea. (Photo by Chung Sung-Jun/Getty Images)

Visit H.W. Wilson's Web site: www.hwwilson.com

Printed in the United States of America

Contents

Preface

In 1984, more than a decade before the Internet became available to anyone with access to a computer and a modem, the novelist Thomas Pynchon recognized that emerging technologies had the potential to change the relationship between individuals and those in power. Asking "Is It O.K. to Be a Luddite?" Pynchon implicitly compared the political implications of today's computer revolution to the 19th century's Industrial Revolution (see Appendix). While he speculated that computers would provide the means for ordinary individuals to challenge mainstream avenues of power, Pynchon offered a vivid counterargument to the view that increased technology would lead to less freedom, a dogma exemplified by George Orwell's *1984*, a novel about a world in which technology has given rise to an all-pervasive totalitarian government known as Big Brother.

Since the Industrial Revolution, thanks in part to the Luddites, challenges to ruling elites have often been cast in terms of challenges to technology. After technological advances in England made their jobs in textile factories obsolete, the Luddites—influenced by the actions of a man named Ned Lud in the 18th century—banded together between 1811 and 1816 to destroy the machines that were robbing them of their livelihood. The term *Luddite* has since come to refer to anyone hostile to advances in technology and can—and often does—connote one opposed to those in control of that technology. "But we now live, we are told, in the Computer Age. What is the outlook for Luddite sensibility? Will mainframes attract the same hostile attention as knitting frames once did? I really doubt it," Pynchon observes. "Machines have already become so user-friendly that even the most unreconstructed of Luddites can be charmed into laying down the old sledgehammer and stroking a few keys instead." The emergence of the new media has made Pynchon's conjectures a large-scale reality—even while making Orwell's worst fears a real possibility. Over the last 10 years, the new media has changed the way people receive and engage with information, allowing those outside the centers of power the opportunity to challenge both corporate and political authorities, all while sitting in front of their computer terminals.

Among the tools most responsible for enabling this new environment are weblogs, or blogs—frequently updated online journals that have allowed private individuals to debate and correct journalists on the national stage—and, more recently, podcasts—broadcasts recorded onto audio files and uploaded onto the World Wide Web for others to download and hear as an alternative to radio programs. Individuals, taking on the role of publisher or broadcaster, can now reach an audience without the help of financial backers and distribution outlets, and those who have done so have had surprising successes. Of course, the new media has changed more than publishing and broadcasting. It has revolutionized the way people participate in politics, entertain themselves, educate themselves and their children, socialize, and shop. These changes do not always pose an obvious affront to those who have traditionally controlled the media, but they have offered the unconnected a chance to widen their influence.

The Internet, by giving everyone access to a potential audience, has weakened top-down structures of control, democratizing the media in a way never before possible. This book explores the transformations brought about by the new media. The first section offers a general consideration of recent developments, opening with five articles that discuss the changes, the possibilities, and the public's responses to them. To balance the emphasis on newness, the section ends with an examination of how our attachments to the latest technological gadgets connect us to traditional modes of life.

The second section turns to the world of publishing, where blogging has played a major role in making the new media a relevant force. Particular selections discuss the blogosphere—the name given to the world of blogs—and examine bloggers' contributions to the news media. The section concludes with two articles about book publishing. The next chapter considers the new media's impact on the entertainment industry and how corporate and private entities compete for the attention of consumers. Rounding out the chapter is an article examining how technology could give rise to a new genre, video game narratives, and another entry discussing the revival of old-fashioned forms of commercialization by entertainment executives in order to finance innovations.

The fourth and fifth chapters look at the notion of *media* in a broader sense and examine the possibilities that new technologies have created for students and educators, as well as the new forms of social interaction that have developed online. Specific articles discuss how online databases improve the research capabilities of students and professionals. Other entries examine social networking Web sites, communally produced publications, such as the online encyclopedia Wikipedia, and new-media shops. New-media developments have also led to certain excesses; consequently, the last section concludes with articles addressing the dangers of the Web.

I would like to thank the authors and publications that granted permission to reprint the articles in this volume. I would also like to acknowledge those who have helped me put this book together, especially Lynn Messina, Paul McCaffrey, Mari Rich, and Jennifer Curry. Of course, nothing would have been possible without John Farris, whose guidance sustains all those who know him. I would also like to thank my wife, Raquel, for her patience.

Albert Rolls
April 2006

I. Changing World: The Emergence of the New Media

Editor's Introduction

Ed Power, a journalist for Ireland's *Sunday Tribune*, wrote in early 2005, "The weblog . . . the internet journal . . . has changed the world? Yes! Blogs have permanently and profoundly redefined the relationship between the individual and the masses. Raising the possibility of a future without a corporate media. Altering the tone of discourse between those who would lead and those who would follow." The assertion, while perhaps overly optimistic, is not without merit. While the corporate media and similar giants are unlikely to fade away, they have been obliged to modify themselves to compete in a world where individuals can engage them on equal ground. Of course, the powerful are not the only entities undergoing a rapid evolution: Individuals are also altering their lifestyles to adapt to the changes wrought by the new media.

The articles that appear in this section explore the relationship between the new media and the worlds of corporations, political parties, and individuals. Larry Williams's "Internet Revolution Is Gaining Momentum" discusses what the Internet-based media has made possible, including blogs, music downloads, and podcasts, and how people are using them. Williams goes on to note, "traditional media giants . . . are expected, ultimately, to dominate the new media," though he suggests they are now obliged to accommodate themselves to the public in ways previously considered unthinkable. Power's "The Blog Revolution and How It Changed the World" outlines the achievements of bloggers—including revelations about the relationship between Monica Lewinsky and Bill Clinton, the arrival of Howard Dean on the national stage during the Democratic primary race, and the discrediting of documents used by CBS News to prove George W. Bush had gone AWOL from the National Guard—to demonstrate their ability to subvert the mainstream media. Power also considers the potential for using blogs as a means of dissent in countries that lack the freedoms enjoyed in the United States and suggests that even if the old-media giants retain their dominance, the masses are no longer passive enough to be dictated to.

Micah L. Sifry explores the latter notion as it applies to the U.S. political landscape in "The Rise of Open-Source Politics." With the airways more accessible to individuals, they now have the means to make their voices heard. "The era of top-down politics—where campaigns, institutions and journalism were cloistered communities powered by hard-to-amass capital—is over," Sifry contends. He goes on to examine how Howard Dean's presidential campaign, though it failed to propel the candidate into the White House, marked the beginning of a more collaborative approach to political organizing, one that enabled voter participation through Internet communities and led to a closer relationship between the candidates and the electorate. Sifry argues that the future of politics lies on the Web, even while calling attention to problems—such as the divide separating those with Internet access (primarily upper-class white male voters) and those without. In "Standing Corrected" Sean Dodson reports on a project that employed the collaborative nature of the Internet for a different purpose, telling the story of Dan Gillmor, a journalist who posted drafts of a book about the media on which he was working onto his blog and solicited advice from readers. The result is a text whose very creation subverts the division between producer and consumer, a phenomenon that Gillmor argues is one of the characteristics that distinguishes the new media from the old.

Taking a wider look at the social changes produced by access to the World Wide Web, Jonathan J. H. Zhu and Enhai Wang's "Diffusion, Use, and Effect of the Internet in China" investigates the speed with which Internet use has increased in China, reporting on changes in the population's habits and proposing that these changes are similar to those that occurred in other nations after the introduction of the Internet. By examining the Chinese public's response to the outbreak of Severe Acute Respiratory Syndrome (SARS), Zhu and Wang demonstrate how the Web has enabled people in China to circumvent official channels of information.

Ana Veciana-Suarez's "Growing Up Online" returns us to America, focusing on how Internet use among young people, particularly the availability of Instant Messaging, is altering the experience of growing up, exposing today's youth to realities from which previous generations were more easily sheltered. Veciana-Suarez, however, does find similarities between the present generation and earlier ones, even though the medium through which they express themselves has changed. The new generation of Web-savvy adults, Douglas Rushkoff suggests in "It's Got a Hold on You," also shares commonalities with previous generations, as well as others who prefer not to utilize high technology. When discussing the more sophisticated gadgets, cell phones in particular, Rushkoff argues that these devices serve the same function as totemic objects in earlier times. "On an anthropological level," he observes, "we humans can't help but relate to their immense power with a bit of fear, reverence and mystery." The high-tech objects so many of us hold dear today may be different from those items people valued in the past, but the impulses that compel us to endow them with importance remain the same.

Internet Revolution Is Gaining Momentum

By Larry Williams
The Baltimore Sun, July 3, 2005

Last Monday morning, after the U.S. Supreme Court announced its decision to rein in the illegal sharing of music files on the Web, the Internet was humming with the news.

On SCOTUSblog, a Web site sponsored by a Washington law firm, Lyle Denniston, a veteran legal journalist, was posting the news and analysis while an array of legal experts offered their views of what the court had decided.

Reports on the court's decision appeared on the home pages of millions of Internet users linked to their favorite news sources by RSS reader software. Others were listening to analysis of the court's decisions on podcasts downloaded from the Web.

There is still lots on the Web to complain about—from poor security to spam and pop-up ads to balky e-mail and browser programs. Despite all that, the Web is in the midst of a revolution—evolving rapidly into an increasingly sophisticated and useful tool for living.

There are two important reasons for the gains. More than half of all at-home Internet users have high-speed connections, and there has been a rapid development of software tools to help users manage the vast sea of Internet media.

Once limited by slow downloads and inadequate Web tools, users are now able to do much more.

As a consequence, more and more people are going online to view, listen or download a wide array of media, to play games, to shop at increasingly elaborate Web sites, to read the news, contribute to blogs, share photos and, of course, to chat online, frequently with a camera turned on.

About 67 percent of all Americans now use the Web, says a survey by the Pew Internet & American Life Project taken in February and March. User demographics are impressive, the survey indicates. About 84 percent of all 18-to-29-year-olds now get online, as do 89 percent of college graduates and 85 percent of those earning $50,000 to $75,000.

Internet commerce is continuing to grow at a double-digit pace as do the profits and business potential of Google and other online companies. Nearly $10 billion was spent on Internet advertising last year, and sales on the Internet increased in the first quarter of this year increased to nearly $20 billion, nearly 24 percent higher than in the corresponding period of 2004, the Census Bureau reported in May.

Enthusiasm about the growing economic power of the Internet has helped Google's stock price climb from under $100 a share when the company went public last summer to nearly $300 a share last week.

In fact, some observers reflecting on the collapse of the dot.com bubble in 2000 are viewing the skyrocketing value of Google's stock with alarm. Some experts say the future might be more challenging as Internet companies compete for the attention of users.

But others say the real fun is just beginning.

Last week, Yahoo, one of the Web's most popular home bases, announced a new service called MyWeb2.0 that allows users to collect favorite Web sites and share them with friends or co-workers.

As more and more people migrate to the Internet for their entertainment, traditional media giants are following.

Also last week, Apple Computer Inc. announced that a new directory would be provided on its iTunes Web site that would allow users to find and download favorite podcasts—radio shows and other audio programs posted on the Internet. Another Pew survey indicated 6 million Americans have listened to podcasts.

Not be left behind, Google announced last week that it will make available a free version of its Google Earth software program that permits users to view high-resolution digital imagery of the planet.

One possible use of the new software would be to mark the locations of local restaurants or real estate listings on a photo map of a community using a link to a database.

When it comes to music and movies, experts predict that the Supreme Court's decision will do little to inhibit illegal file-swapping. A national survey of adult Internet users taken this year seems to confirm that view. Some 57 percent of high-speed Internet users told Pew they believe there is not much the government can do to reduce illegal file-sharing.

The exchange of music and movie files isn't limited to file-sharing networks. About 19 percent of music and video downloaders (about 7 million adults) say they have downloaded files from someone else's iPod or MP3 player. About 28 percent (roughly 10 million people) say they get files by e-mail and instant messages.

But as more and more people migrate to the Internet for their entertainment, traditional media giants are following and are expected, ultimately, to dominate the new media, with sales of downloadable movies, made-for-Internet broadcast material and news.

Apple Computer is showing the way. The company has sold more than 400 million songs from it's online iTunes music store to fill the 15 million iPod personal music players it has sold worldwide.

On Thursday, the company put out a news release reporting that its iTunes customers had subscribed to more than 1 million podcasts from the new podcast directory.

And newspaper editors fretting about declining circulation can take heart from yet another Pew study released last week reporting that that fully 62 percent of Internet news consumers say they read the Web sites of local or national newspapers.

"Convenience is more important than cost in explaining why many Americans are reading the paper online instead of in print," said Pew's Lee Rainie. "Among those who say they read the Web version of the newspaper, 73 percent cite convenience compared with just 8 percent who do so because it is free."

Pew calls the online newspaper audience "mostly male, wealthy and highly educated."

New software tools are fast making it possible for people to easily organize a flow of up-to-the minute reports from wide array of sources, including traditional media, blogs and other specialized Web sites.

Improved search engines from Google, Yahoo, Microsoft and others are making it much easier and safer to find everything from useful Web sites to academic research to wireless hot spots, a useful book or an interesting dinner date.

These same companies are offering custom home pages that include personal mail service with seemingly unlimited mail storage, local TV and movie listings, customized news, weather and sports reports and easy to manage storage for other media, including personal blogs, photos, home movies, maps and sound recordings.

Blogs, sites set up by individuals or institutions to discuss issues or share information, are proliferating like stars in the sky.

Flickr, an online photo-storage site, is another example how people can use the Web to help get their lives in order. Users can store personal photos on the Flickr site and share them with family and friends who check the site or the world if they like.

There is even a blog site that explains how to combine Flickr with Google Maps to create a map linking locations where images were captured with the images themselves.

Some of this seems more than a little silly at times, even dedicated Webbers agree. That's the point, they say, once you have a high-speed connection and a computer most of the play is free.

In a more serious vein, a number of efforts are under way to provide better guides to the most useful and reliable sites on the Web.

Google and Yahoo are offering comprehensive guides to the Web and the Open Directory Project (dmoz.org) is building a comprehensive guide to the best of the Web using an army of volunteer editors.

Google hopes to build a comprehensive Web library through a years-long project of scanning the contents of important university libraries across the nation. And Yahoo is offering an online directory for Internet-posted academic research that can be searched by university or topic.

The next big challenge, for the founders of the fast-evolving Internet is to lower the costs of high-speed access, so the less affluent can benefit from access. Amazingly, the United States lags behind many other countries in providing low-cost, high-speed Internet access.

And some worry that another Supreme Court decision last week—a ruling that freed cable television companies a requirement that forces local phone companies to provide access to other Internet service marketers—could lead to less competition and higher prices for high-speed Internet service.

The cure for that could be high-speed wireless Internet service like that now offered in some coffee shops and libraries and coffee shops. There's a new version of wireless that could offer low-cost service across cities.

The Growth of the Internet

Yahoo—My Web 2.0

A new web site that helps you organize your favorite Web pages and share them with friends or coworkers at myweb.search.yahoo.com.

Flickr

Allows you to share photographs with friends or the world or to study public and private images posted by others. Tags help keep this bounty organized and every image is free to anyone who would like to make a copy at www.flickr.com.

Podcast Directory

Apple announced that it intends to offer a directory to help users find some of the 20,000 audio programs available on the Internet for downloading. In addition to NBC and ABC news programs, podcast listeners can hear Rush Limbaugh, Al Franken and a host of others, including lots of music.

Google World

Google announced last week that it would make available a free version of its Google Earth software program that permits users to view high-resolution digital images of the planet. Users will be able to create images that include useful details.

Wikipedia

A mostly reliable and wildly popular online encyclopedia that has been created by its faithful users at en.wikipedia.org.

The Blog Revolution and How It Changed the World

By Ed Power
The Sunday Tribune (Ireland), February 6, 2005

They influence US presidential elections, make millions for savvy companies and reveal the intimate secrets of a callgirl. And there are eight million of them. Blogs, web diaries to the uninitiated, have changed the way we see the world.

REVOLUTIONS were never supposed to be like this. Subtle, wordy, GEEKY. These aren't the adjectives we expected to be reaching for as society tipped on its axis. Yet that is exactly how blogging has changed the world . . . quietly and politely, almost without your noticing. Hot blood and gunpowder have rarely achieved so much.

The weblog . . . the internet journal . . . has changed the world? Yes! Blogs have permanently and profoundly redefined the relationship between the individual and the masses. Raising the possibility of a future without a corporate media. Altering the tone of discourse between those who would lead and those who would follow. Oh, and they've made the web a heck of a more interesting place in which to hang out.

Blogging's emerging influence is underlined with the recent publication of *Belle De Jour*, a novel adapted from the anonymous (and some claim fictional) blog of a London callgirl.

When it seeped onto the net early last year, *Belle* became instantly sensational, setting the London media in particular tittering like school girls. Who was this wry mistress of the forbidden? Could she be real? Or was she the alterego of a would-be novelist or perhaps of an established writer, attempting to escape a pigeon-hole?

Rumours flew like champagne corks in Lillie's Bordello.

Writer Toby Young was fingered as Belle (he denied it). Sarah Champion, an unpublished novelist who in the mid 1990s gained some celebrity as editor of the 'e-generation' anthology *Disco Biscuits*, was a suspect. The louder her denials, the greater media watchers' inclination to disbelieve them.

Eventually, some even starting to suspect Belle of being a real person.

The truth is in there What is indisputable is that *Belle De Jour* marks a watershed in the mainstreaming of blogging. Without having to woo a publisher or court an agent, the author has stormed the literary salon. They didn't have to follow the rules because in the blogosphere there are no rules. There is only the limits of your ability and your hunger.

> *How has blogging changed the world? In too many ways to articulate adequately.*

To claim that blogging has tumbled the walls between the creators and consumers of media may strike you as a portentous brag for a pursuit that has yet to offload the fan boy tag. Sure, *Belle De Jour* is an exception . . . (literally) one in 10 million. Nobody denies that 99% of blogs tend towards indulgent dross, churned out by writers who remain amateur for the straightforward reason that they aren't very good.

But then, to paraphrase the science fiction author Harlan Ellison, 99% of everything is crap. The bloggers who matter may comprise only a tiny percentile, yet the breadth of their achievements . . . the possibilities raised by those achievements . . . justifies the hyperbole.

How has blogging changed the world? In too many ways to articulate adequately. Most blatantly, blogging has put the mass media on notice: no longer will we . . . the IT-literate masses . . . consume your produce without question.

"Blogging has caused significant changes, chiefly in news, " says Eddie Brennan, a lecturer in media studies at Dublin Institute of Technology.

"Blogging has brought stories into mainstream media which otherwise might not have seen the light of day. A good example here is the Drudge Report, by Matt Drudge, and its exposés on Clinton and Monica Lewinsky. Significantly, these stories were not confirmed by independent sources but after they were propagated by Drudge they found their way into the mainstream news agenda. This was chiefly out of fear of competing media grabbing a scoop. Here you had a blog influencing the mainstream agenda."

Outcome aside, the story of last year's US presidential face-off was the arrival of blogging as a cultural force. In a country where traditional news organisations seemed to shrink from controversy (as though it were contagious), the wave of election blogs felt like a spike of righteous vitriol in your veins.

However, blogging did more than add pep to the campaign, making it seem less like a waxwork approximation of democracy. Howard Dean, the Democrat governor of Vermont, raced into the favourite's position in the primaries thanks, in some part, to cheerleaders in the blogging community (his status as an underground favourite ultimately dooming him to be Kerry's pace-setter).

And it was bloggers who initially debunked falsified documents which, according to CBS News, proved President Bush had gone awol during national service.

We now know that the network had aired the story despite huge inconsistencies in its source material. Without the outcry . . . and the dogged research . . . of bloggers, would the forgery have been exposed?

In America, if you want to dig deep, you call a blogger.

Pinning down the truth sometimes requires obsessional, even maniacal, devotion, a quality the American media has lately rejected as a pointless diversion of resources that might otherwise be invested in speculating the who, what and why of Brad 'n' Jen's break-up. In America, if you want to dig deep, you call a blogger.

For left-wingers, blogging provided a crucial outlet as election day loomed. Pro-Kerry blogs such as Daily Kos and Wonkette drew hundreds of thousands of surfers and created a fallow environment for discourse. With their right-wing peers shunting oxygen into the "Swift Boats Veterans For Truth" smear campaign against Kerry, liberal outrage helped temper the discourse.

The blue-state nightmare of a second Bush term became reality all the same of course. Yet blogging has provided leftist America with a forum were it could "out" itself without fear of vilification. In 2004, the heartbeat of US radicalism was to be discovered, thumping and urgent, on the web.

Dissenting Voices

In societies with far less freedom than the United States (they exist, no matter what the anti-war hardcore would like you to believe), blogging has assumed a prime role for dissidents.

During the Iraq war, bloggers offered a more articulate and accurate account of the population's terror and confusion than the ranks of embedded media riding on the coattails of the Coalition military. It was "Baghdad blogger" Salman Pax who most credibly narrated the toppling of Saddam Hussein. Huddled in his city-centre apartment, blogging while the bombs rained down, Pax delivered what was arguably a far truer insight into life on the front line than the reporters rushing towards the conflict zone.

Blogs are also a wellspring of dissent in Iran. Farsi is the fourth most common language for keeping an online journal, with Iranians responsible for more than 75,000 blogs.

In a country where 100 media organisations and 41 daily newspapers have been shut by the state in the past five years, blogging has become the vernacular for political discourse.

Like invisible scavengers, Iran's bloggers inevitably sniff out banned materials and post them on the internet. You can even download hand-typed abstracts from the *Satanic Verses* by Salman Rushdie, who was the subject of a fatwa, issued by the late Ayatollah Khomeini.

In the aftermath of the earthquake in Bam, which caused 20,000 deaths, the Iranian weblog community played a central role in the rescue operation. Bloggers arranged their own collection points and the transportation of aid; notified their virtual community of the whereabouts of survivors relocated to hospitals in urban centres; organised hospital visits, charity sales and recruited volunteers.

The inevitable state backlash began last year, when Sina Motallebi, a web-based journalist, became the first blogger in the world to be imprisoned for his activities. A wider clampdown followed, as the authorities moved against online media. "In a country where the independent press has to fight for its survival on a daily basis, online publications and weblogs are the last media to fall into the authorities' clutches," says an analysis of media freedom in Iran by Reporters sans Frontieres (RSF). "Through arrests and intimidation, the Iranian authorities are now trying to spread terror among online journalists."

> *"I don't think blogging can have a big impact in Ireland, yet, but someday it certainly will."*—John Fay, editor of the blog Irish Eagle

Recently, it was reported that the Tehran government is seeking to establish a national intranet, which would effectively wall-off Iran from the web. However, the failure of similar efforts in China . . . now home to a flourishing blogsphere . . . suggest the freedoms offered by modern technology are not easily suppressed.

For obvious reasons, the Irish blogosphere is a less radical neighbourhood. Political activism in fact is often the last thing on its mind (with the notable exception of a clutch of Northern Ireland blogs). One reason, surely, is the technophile bent of many Irish bloggers. To outsiders, their monosyllabic musings on the IT industry may as well be in a made-up language. The odd buzzword, the occasional phrase, may register but mostly it feels as though you're ploughing through advanced-Klingon. To a newcomer, Irish blogging feels like an intimidating environment.

"I don't think blogging can have a big impact in Ireland, yet, but someday it certainly will," agrees John Fay, editor of the Irish Eagle, a blog with a quasi-political theme. "Blogging today is like pirate radio in its early days. Eventually, I think blogging will be able to make a real impact, but by that time blogging will have been co-opted into the mass media. Blogs are mostly written by and for people who represent a niche (or more accurately, niches) not represented by the mainstream media."

Yet we shouldn't be so quick to disdain the Irish geek-osphere. Dry and impenetrable as they are, Irish blogs that mull over technology's bleeding edges, deliver a palpable sense of the future unfurling.

"Blogging is like watching the thought processes of society at work; fascinating, and very informative," says Clive Thompson, a blogger who writes about technology for *The New York Times*. "Blogs are an interesting way to track what's popular . . . a way of seeing which ideas, memes, trends and news events are getting the most comment."

Media Bloglash

Blogging's role in the creation of a fresh media vernacular is not universally celebrated however. In fact, observe closely and you may even detect the stirrings of a backlash (or should that be bloglash?).

Sceptics argue that, though bloggers are often first on the scene, they employ standards which are far less rigorous than those of conventional news-gatherers. Like a witch mulling over a toxic preparation, Matt Drudge, editor of the right-wing Drudge Report, has in particular been accused of mingling fact and fiction, rumour and poisonous secondguesses.

"Of course, people like Drudge do not operate in isolation. His rise to fame cannot be separated from Republicans' animosity towards Clinton and the intention to politically damage him in any way possible. If there had been less opposition among Republicans and sympathetic media these stories might not have made the impression they did," says Eddie Brennan.

"Despite such changes there is a lot of hype about blogging. They are not of any consequence for most people in their everyday media consumption. Their chief significance is in the way they are reported to the general public by the mainstream media. Many journalists now create the impression that blogs may be the new journalism. This is akin to the irrational dotcom hype of the mid- to late-'90s."

The suspicion that blogging will be absorbed by rather than conquer the media is a theme echoed by Jack Shafer, executive editor of *Slate* magazine.

"I think most practising journalists today are as webby as any blogger you care to name," he wrote in *Slate* recently. "Journalists have had access to broadband connections for longer than most civilians, and nearly every story they tackle begins with a web dump of essential information from Google or a proprietary database such as Nexis or Factiva.

They conduct interviews via email, download official documents from .gov sites, check facts, and monitor the competition . . . including blogs . . . the whole while."

For hundreds of thousands of bloggers however, politics and cultural issues hardly ever intrude. In the blogosphere, science fiction fans, wannabe novelists, rock devotees and countless others chatter politely among themselves. They don't want to change the world. They just want to know what you thought of last night's *Stargate*.

Celebrities, too, have seized on blogging. Famous people are often convinced that the media is bent on distorting their words. With blogging, they may hold forth with impunity, delivering "their" truth without fear of being misconstrued.

Thus dance-artist Moby can extol us to save the world by renouncing meat, former Smashing Pumpkins' leader Billy Corgan is able to re-ignite his feud with ex-band mates and techno-savvy footballers may diss their managers, clubs and fans. It's like *Celebrity Big Brother* with no time-limit or offswitch.

Blogging on the Job

A notable recent phenomenon has been the work blog. If you have ever wondered how it feels to flip burgers all day . . . or if you DO flip burgers and could do with a little empathy . . . the work blog is on hand to sate your curiosity.

Work bloggers who have achieved a profile include Diary Of A Fast Food Life (that would be the burger-flipper), supermarket shelf-stackers and advertising executives (My Life As a Liar), Professor B, who writes Bitch PhD, uses her blog "to work out my incredible anxieties over my academic identity, and to put those anxieties out there in a public forum because a lot of people feel them."

Critical mass, of a sort, was achieved by workblogs last year when Waterstones in the UK sacked an employee for grousing about work in his blog. Delta Airlines took a similarly unforgiving view after a stewardess posted photos of herself in uniform on her blog.

Yet rather than recoil from bloggers, the corporate world is increasingly attempting to convert them to their cause.

Olympus, for example, has devised a new marketing strategy to embrace the medium. Whenever a new camera is nearing launch, snippets of information are passed on to popular blogs. The company believes flirting with bloggers helps generate interest in addition to providing early feedback on what the public thinks of the new model. Chatter from the blogs, Olympus says, will reveal more than any amount of market research.

In fact, blogs have become so powerful they already have the launch of a company to their credit. Kathy Rittweger, chief of online information service Blinkx, was on what she thought was just a normal trip to the offices of *Business 2.0* magazine to show the editor her new search software. Om Malik, one of the journalists at the meeting, was sufficiently impressed that he immediately wrote about it on his blog.

"He called me to say he'd done a 'blog' on us and I have to confess I was disappointed as it didn't sound as good as an article," Rittweger said last year. "Within a couple of hours we were being mentioned on thousands of sites and I had venture capitalists calling me left, right and centre. The blog made us so popular that we had to bring forward our launch from autumn to June."

The publication of *Belle De Jour* will be hailed as a further vindication of blogging. Regardless of their identity, the author would almost certainly be toiling in anonymity still had blogging not offered the potential for instant publishing.

In much the same way that punk rock embodied an "anyone-can-do-it" outlook, blogging puts the web in the hands of its citizenry. It is an incurably democratic means of expression. Puny technical know-how is required. All you need is a computer . . . or the address of a good cybercafe . . . and something you believe worth saying.

Eight million blogs are estimated to share the internet (those with an interest have long since been forced to give up keeping count). There is room for another eight million.

Only a fraction of a percent will ever be worth reading. But who is to say . . . perhaps yours will be one of them? In the blogosphere, everyone's voice holds equal weight. Could it be that it's your turn to stand on the roof-slates and scream your lungs dry?

The Rise of Open-Source Politics

By Micah L. Sifry
The Nation, November 22, 2004

Whether you're a Democrat in mourning or a Republican in glee, the results from election day should not obscure an important shift in America's civic life. New tools and practices born on the Internet have reached critical mass, enabling ordinary people to participate in processes that used to be closed to them. It may seem like cold comfort for Kerry supporters now, but the truth is that voters don't have to rely on elected or self-appointed leaders to chart the way forward anymore. The era of top-down politics—where campaigns, institutions and journalism were cloistered communities powered by hard-to-amass capital—is over. Something wilder, more engaging and infinitely more satisfying to individual participants is arising alongside the old order.

One moment when this new power began to be collectively understood by grassroots activists was on April 23, 2003. It was 4:31 pm (EST) in cyberspace when Mathew Gross, then toiling in obscurity on Howard Dean's presidential campaign, posted the following missive on the message board of SmirkingChimp.com, a little-known but heavily trafficked forum for anti-Bush sentiment:

> So I wander back to my desk and there really IS a note on my chair from Joe Trippi, the Campaign Manager for Howard Dean. The note says:
> *Matt, Start an "Ask the Dean Campaign" thread over at the Smirking Chimp.—Joe*
> Surely a seminal moment in Presidential politics, no?
> So, here's the deal. Use this space to throw questions and comments our way. I'll be checking this thread, Joe will be checking this thread. We're understandably very busy so don't give up if we disappear for a day or two. Talk amongst yourselves while we're out of the room, as it were. But we will check in and try to answer questions. We want to hear from you. We want to know what you think.
> So, go to it. And thanks for supporting Howard Dean.

About an hour later, after thirty responses appeared, Zephyr Teachout, Gross's colleague, chimed in with some answers. A little later, a participant on the site wrote: "This is too cool, an actual direct line to the Dean campaign committee! Pinch me—I must be dreaming!" Ultimately, more than 400 people posted comments on

---

Gross's thread. Richard Hoefer, a frequent visitor, later wrote me: "That was an amazing day to see that rise out of nowhere. People were floored that the thread title was 'Ask the Dean Campaign'— and Trippi and Matt were actually asking questions and interacting. Never before had anyone seen that."

Never before had the top-down world of presidential campaigning been opened to a bottom-up, laterally networked community of ordinary voters. The Smirking Chimp is a website with 25,000-plus registered members, founded after the 2000 election as a gathering place for liberals, progressives and leftists who felt the newly selected President reminded them most of, well, a smirking chimp. Each day they devour and critique the handful of critical articles selected by its webmaster, Jeff Tiedrich, a New York–based programmer who started the site on a lark and is amazed by its growth. "The community of the Chimp is the angry, angry, engaged left," Tiedrich says. When it was offered a direct connection to Dean, who was then the only candidate attacking Bush and the war in stark terms, lightning struck.

"The reason these community sites have formed," says Gross, rattling off the names DailyKos, MyDD, Eschaton, Democratic Underground and Buzzflash, along with the Smirking Chimp, "is the Democratic Party is too based on insiders." (Some Republicans apparently feel the same way, and have started similar sites, like RedState.org.) Indeed, at most political organizations, "membership" and "participation" mean little more than writing a check in response to a direct-mail appeal, as Harvard professor Theda Skocpol argues in her 2003 book *Diminished Democracy*. This wasn't always the case, Skocpol notes—through the first half of the 1900s tens of millions of Americans were engaged in cross-class fellowship and civic activism through federated mass membership organizations like the Free Masons, the Knights of Pythias and the American Legion. But, undermined by the Vietnam War, the "rights revolutions" and especially the new mass-media system, mass membership groups atrophied. They were replaced by a proliferating array of professionally run, top-down advocacy organizations, like the AARP and Natural Resources Defense Council. "America is now full of civic entrepreneurs who are constantly looking upward for potential angels, shmoozing with the wealthy," Skocpol writes, rather than talking to people of modest means.

But it is also true that insiderism and elitism have recently come under heavy attack, as everyone from Trent Lott to Dan Rather can attest. And it's not just Congress and big media whose hierarchies are being challenged; nonprofits and interest groups are feeling the ground shift too. "Members Unite! You have nothing to lose but your newsletters and crappy coffee-cup premiums," read the title of a recent post on WorldChanging.com, a blog devoted to fostering this movement. New web-based tools are facilitating a different way of doing politics, one in which we may all actually, not hypothetically, be equals; where transparency and accountability are more than slogans; and where anyone with few resources but a compelling message can be a community organizer, an ad-maker, a reporter, a publisher, a theorist, a money-raiser or a leader.

Consider these harbingers:

- About two-thirds of American adults use the Internet, and more than 55 percent have access to a high-speed Internet connection at either home or work.

- More than 53 million people have contributed material online, according to a spring 2003 survey by the Pew Internet & American Life Project.

- More than 15 million have their own website.

- A new blog, or online journal, is created every 5.3 seconds, according to Technorati.com, a site that tracks the known universe of these easily updated websites. As of November 1, there were almost 4.3 million blogs, a million more than three months before. More than half of them are regularly updated by their creators, producing more than 400,000 fresh postings every day. (Full disclosure: My brother David is the founder of Technorati.)

- A well-written blog, Joshua Micah Marshall's Talking Points Memo, gets more than 500,000 monthly visitors—as many as the entire website of *The American Prospect*, the magazine where Marshall used to work, at a fraction of the cost.

- Of the approximately 400,000–500,000 people who attended a political meeting through the social-networking site Meetup.com this election season, half had never gone to a political meeting before. Sixty percent were under 40.

- Attendees of Meetups for Democratic Party presidential candidates reported making an average of $312 in political contributions last year.

- A two-minute political cartoon lampooning both Kerry and Bush, put out by JibJab.com this past summer, had 10 million viewings in the month of July—three times the number of hits on both presidential campaign websites combined—and has since been viewed another 55 million times.

But it isn't the quantity of interactions taking place that suggests the change under way; it is the quality of those conversations. If, as a *New Yorker* cartoon put it, "On the Internet, no one knows if you're a dog," on the Internet, no one likes it if you don't speak in a genuine human voice. Says Christopher Locke, one of the co-authors of *The Cluetrain Manifesto*, a bible of sorts for business people trying to understand how the Internet is changing commerce:

> Compared to this kind of personal, intimate, knowledgeable and highly engaged voice . . . top-down corporate communications come across as stale and stentorian—the boring, authoritarian voice of command and control. The glaring difference between

these styles is the strange attractor that has brought tens of millions flocking to the Internet. There's new life passing along the wires. And it hasn't been coming from corporations.

Nor has it been coming from politicians, not until recently.

It's the Network, Stupid

The differences between MoveOn.org, the big, liberal e-mail activist group, and DailyKos.com, the biggest of the new blog-centered sites, are illustrative. MoveOn and its associated PAC give its 2.8 million subscribers lots of easy, timely and mostly well-chosen options to get involved in national affairs. Most people are too busy to get deeply involved in many issues, and thus many respond positively to a request for help if action is one click away. MoveOn's sheer size makes small actions feel larger—maybe you'll do a bake sale for democracy if you know 10,000 other people are doing it too. It has raised millions of dollars for political candidates and advertising, and involved its subscribers in many innovative experiments, like its June 2003 online presidential primary and its "Bush in 30 Seconds" ad contest.

Many respond positively to a request for help if action is one click away.

But MoveOn is still very much a top-down organization. Technologist and organizational strategist Tom Mandel says, "MoveOn is to liberal politics as Wal-Mart is to retail." Wes Boyd, Joan Blades, Eli Pariser and the other members of its leadership team may sign all their mass e-mails with their first names, but they set policy for the organization in much the same way as every other nonprofit, by talking among themselves, fielding proposals from various suitors, polling their audience and talking among themselves some more. Periodically they will ask subscribers to offer their ideas about priorities using an "ActionForum" program that enables visitors to suggest an issue, read what others have said and vote on their preferences. But that tool gives MoveOn members little ability to talk to each other directly or to aggregate their ideas independently of the choices its leaders make for them.

By comparison, DailyKos is a multilayered community engineered to reward ideas that bubble up from below. Like many bloggers, Markos Moulitsas, the Gulf War veteran who runs it, requires visitors to register (for free) if they want to post a comment. He also encourages users to set up their own "diaries," or blogs within his blog, where they can post their own entries. Unlike most blogs, the DailyKos is built on a tool called Scoop, which includes peer moderation, where members rank each other's entries and comments. Smart diary postings thus often rise to Moulitsas's attention, and if he reprints them on his main page they gain an even larger audience.

In addition, people with high rankings become "trusted users" who have the ability to recommend that visitors who try to disrupt conversations or simply post right-wing taunts be banned from the site. Only Moulitsas has the power to make that decision, and he weeds his garden carefully. "If somebody posts and I haven't seen them in a while," he told me, "I'll say, 'Where've you been?'" Amazingly, he insists that he has developed personal relationships with hundreds of people. "That's what happens after two years of reading the same names over and over again," he says.

> *Blog-based political networking has had all kinds of concrete political effects.*

As a result, the Kos community has become a very efficient collaboration engine—not only for pooling money for candidates (at least $600,000 has been given through the site) but also for rapid fact-checking of political statements and news stories, quick dissemination of news of voting irregularities and brainstorming of campaign themes. During the presidential debates, Kos's daily traffic surged to more than a half million visits. The DailyKos, to be sure, is still an egocentric organization dominated by one person who is not without blemishes, like refusing to disclose who his paying political clients are. But his success shows the power of an open network approach to organizing.

Beyond Kos, blog-based political networking has had all kinds of concrete political effects. Best known is the way prominent bloggers like Joshua Micah Marshall, along with some conservatives like Glenn Reynolds, fired up the Trent Lott–Strom Thurmond story, which led to Lott's fall from grace. More recently, bloggers have spurred the resignation of a homophobic Congressman (Ed Schrock), undermined the credibility of key evidence in Dan Rather's story on Bush's National Guard service, distributed Jon Stewart's blistering October 15 appearance on CNN's *Crossfire*, beat back Sinclair Broadcasting's plan to force its stations to air an anti-Kerry documentary, and formed a back channel for unhappy soldiers in Iraq and their families back home.

The new political technology works because it gives individuals a way to pool their time, attention and resources around causes they may hold in common—and to do it without needing to become a professional activist or wait for approval from any authority figure. "It's not about the technology or the blog," says Mathew Gross now. "It's about having a conversation and treating people with respect."

The New Gold Rush

If conventional politicos had doubts about that proposition after Dean's late-January collapse in the Democratic primaries, their questions were muted a few weeks later, when a $2,000 investment in advertising on a few political blogs generated more than $80,000 two weeks later in small contributions to Democratic Congressional candidate Ben Chandler. Chandler went on to win the special election for the 6th District in Kentucky. Suddenly politicians were adding community-building tools to their websites and buying ads on popular blogs. For firms that specialize in selling Internet plumbing and the expertise needed to run it, like GetActive, Issue Dynamics, CTSG, Groundspring, IStandFor, Right Click Strategies, Kintera and Convio, these are flush times.

In late March an audience of several hundred technologists, venture capitalists and journalists gathered at Esther Dyson's annual PC Forum in Scottsdale, Arizona, a top venue for the computer industry. This year the hot topic was social software. The crowd listened intently as Bob Epstein, a member of GetActive's board of directors, told them that the company's clients—groups like Oxfam America, Earthjustice, Riverkeeper, PBS and the AFL-CIO—were seeing huge jumps in online fundraising. Noting that $70 billion is spent every year on direct mail and "some of that will move online," he reassured the crowd that "our goal isn't to change the political system, it's to get a good return on the dollar."

That seemed to be the main focus, too, at the "Politics Online" conference at George Washington University in April. To most of the audience, which was thick with consultants from both parties, the Internet is just a new place for a more sophisticated kind of direct mail, the kind where each solicitation message can be tailored precisely to a voter's concerns and foibles, and where a dribble of quasi participation ("Become an E-Captain!" "Click Here to E-Mail This Pre-Written Message to Your Member of Congress") can produce a torrent of donations.

It fell to David Weinberger, a co-author of the *Cluetrain Manifesto* and an Internet adviser to the Dean campaign, to try to pierce the marketing talk at the conference with a harder truth. "I am not a 'customer' and I am not a 'consumer,'" he fumed during a panel with representatives of MoveOn.org and RightMarch.com over the issue of how best to manage online campaigns. "I am a citizen and a voter. I flee from 'message.' It is advertising. I want to avoid advertising," he roared. Recalling the hullabaloo over Kerry's comment that the Bush campaigners "are the most crooked, lying group I've ever seen," caught when he thought a mike he was wearing was off, Weinberger insisted that this was the best thing that had happened to Kerry. "That was the first time he had been allowed to speak as a human being." Speaking off-mike, he argued, was like blogging—in both cases people's real voices could be heard, which is what we hunger for. "Control kills scale. Control kills passion. Control kills the human voice," Weinberger insisted.

Loss of Control Freaks

That message has been very slow in reaching the Democratic establishment. On his blog, Weinberger tells of meeting DNC chair Terry McAuliffe at a cocktail party. "I tried to say that the Net can do things for campaigns other than raise money . . . for example, bring in a portion of the population that is feeling a tad alienated in part because of the relentless money 'n' marketing focus of the campaign. McAuliffe agreed, and then went on to re-express my point in terms of using the Net to raise money." Nor did this message penetrate the Kerry campaign. "They don't take part in the conversation on the Kerry blog," complained Mathew Gross this past summer. "They're still sort of issuing press releases, albeit in a more human voice."

That's because top-down politics is all about maintaining control. "Think of an established brand with a lot invested in control of its image," says Jonah Seiger, founding partner of Connections Media and a veteran of Internet politicking since the late 1980s. "The idea of opening that up is scary."

"Anybody who does politics the old way will fight doing things the new way because it's harder to get paid for it," says Mark Walsh, CEO of Progress Media, the parent of Air America and a veteran of such companies as VerticalNet and America Online. "Look at every other industry and how the Internet has altered it. Take E-Trade and the selling of stocks. Or Orbitz and the travel industry. In every case, the Internet enables getting rid of the middlemen." For about a year, starting in late 2001, Walsh was McAuliffe's chief technology officer, earning $1 a year to help the Democratic Party upgrade its tech systems. "Terry did want to do the right thing," Walsh says, "but I found the same buzz saw—legacy behavior and consultants who are compensated highly for non-cyber-centric behavior. TV, telemarketing, direct mail—that's where the margins are."

Another veteran of early efforts to convince top Democrats to embrace the new technology, who asked not to be named, said "At the DSCC [Democratic Senatorial Campaign Committee] the executive director, Jim Jordan, flatly didn't care. He said it was in the hands of then-political director Andy Grossman, who said, 'The day someone can show me that the Internet will make a difference in raising money or casting votes, that's the day I will care.'" He said this in 2001—after MoveOn's anti-impeachment campaign, after Jesse Ventura's breakthrough use of the Internet in 1998, after John McCain and Bill Bradley raised millions online in the 2000 primaries.

"The disconnect is now gone," says my source, noting that top Democratic Party staff are all embracing new web-based tools, "but the willingness to acknowledge that change must happen to accompany that is not. The Internet has to become the center of the organization. But the notion of the party's committees having well-defined departments with a top-down hierarchical structure hasn't changed." Walsh adds, "We have to go through a generational purge. People have been fed crap—the McPolitics diet—for so long, the body politic will respond slowly to new tools that will make them smarter and more powerful." Thus one big question for the coming year will be the extent to which grassroots activists, small donors and bloggers decide to raise hard questions about the functioning of the party organs and interest groups that until now have been able to act on their behalf without having to pay a price for their mistakes. The Kerry debacle is a good place to start.

Open-source politics is still a long way off. The term "open source" specifically refers to allowing any software developer to see the underlying source code of a program, so that anyone can analyze it and improve it; better code trumps bad code, and programmers who have proven their smarts have greater credibility and status. Applied to political organizing, open source would mean opening up participation in planning and implementation to the community, letting competing actors evaluate the value of your plans and actions, being able to shift resources away from bad plans and bad planners and toward better ones, and expecting more of participants in return. It would mean moving away from egocentric organizations and toward network-centric organizing.

The Emerging Internet Majority

To the visionary technologists building the new civic software, we are living in nothing short of a paradigm shift. Scott Heiferman, the scrawny, youthful CEO of Meetup.com, enjoys citing Alexis de Tocqueville along with Robert Putnam, and argues, "In the same way that TV took politics away from the grassroots, the Internet will give it back." He predicts a return to the 1800s/early-1900s era of joiners and organizers, when a double-digit level of civic participation in community affairs was common. Steven Johnson, the author of *Emergence*, recently wrote:

> Using open-source coding as a model, it's not a stretch to believe the same process could make politics more representative and fair. Imagine, for example, how a grassroots network could take over some of the duties normally performed by high-priced consultants who try to shape a campaign message that's appealing. If the people receiving the message create it, chances are it's much more likely to stir up passions.

Joi Ito, a Japanese venture capitalist and social entrepreneur, predicts that the web will become more self-organizing and that a new form of "emergent democracy" will evolve that will be more supple and transparent than traditional forms of representative democracy.

There's no question that public discourse is being radically changed. As Dan Gillmor, a technology columnist for the *San Jose Mercury News*, writes in his terrific new book, *We the Media*, "If someone knows something in one place, everyone who cares about that something will know it soon enough." But it's also possible that new Internet-based tools will merely give already advantaged groups greater voice, reinforcing existing inequalities. "I think there are still a lot of Americans who think that no one is listening to them," says Theda Skocpol. She argues that web-enabled politick-ing may just be "really well suited to the liberal side of the spec-trum, where you have a lot of college-educated people who are not connecting to politics through church networks or their workplaces or professional associations, where open partisanship is frowned upon, and where the Democratic Party has fallen into dealing with people as disaggregated individuals, followers or clients, rather than participants."

Indeed, a Bentley College survey of attendees at Meetups for the Democratic presidential candidates and party found they were mostly white middle- and upper-income professionals. According to the Pew Internet and American Life Project's most recent survey, Hispanics have closed the gap with whites, with two-thirds of both groups going online, but Internet usage among blacks lags by about 18 percent. Age is the other obvious predictor of online behavior, with just under one-quarter of people over 65 venturing online. Yet another factor also affects Internet participation: time. "Who is it that spends time online?" asks Mathew Gross. "It's people at home or at desk jobs where they can surf the web. You don't have that kind of time or freedom if you're a dental hygienist or migrant worker," he notes.

People who rely on the net for political information are actually more likely than non-net users to seek out views different from their own.—Pew Internet study

Skocpol argues that the Internet is not changing the class structure of mobilization, because it is all driven by "intentional politics." You have to know in advance that you're looking for political information or to join a con-versation or make a donation before you search on the web, she says. In the past, when federated, mass-mem-bership organizations enlivened civic life, "People didn't have to know in advance that they wanted to be involved," she notes. She has a point: While the web may make it easier for a compelling message to circulate through existing social networks, it doesn't alter our ten-dency to cluster by social group. At the same time, people who rely on the net for political information are actually more likely than non-net users to seek out views different from their own, according to a new Pew Internet study.

These are likely to be momentary bumps in a much larger wave. That's because the next generation is growing up online, rather than adapting to it in their mid-adult years. More than 2 million children aged 6–17 have their own website, according to a December 2003 survey by Grunwald Associates. Twenty-nine percent of kids in grades K–3 have their own e-mail address. Social networking sites like Friendster and Flickr (a photo-sharing site) are drawing millions of participants and fostering new kinds of social conversa-tions, some of which are already political.

Josh Koenig, one of the twenty-somethings who cut their teeth at the Dean campaign and a co-founder of Music for America, says, "We're only seeing the first drips of what is going to be a downpour." When he told me that in most high schools in America, students are using the web to rank their teachers, I thought that was a bit of hyperbole. But then I discovered RateMyTeachers.com, where more than 6 million ratings have been posted by students on more than 900,000 teachers at more than 40,000 American and Canadian middle and high schools. That's triple the number from one year ago, covering about 85 percent of all the schools in both countries.

Just imagine when they take that habit into their adult lives, and start rating other authority figures, like politicians and bosses. The future is in their hands, though the rest of us will be taken along for the ride.

Standing Corrected

By Sean Dodson
Global News Wire, May 13, 2004

Most of us who bother with the matter would admit that the internet is transforming journalism, but how many of us know how far it will go? Dan Gillmor, of the *San Jose Mercury News*, thinks he knows and last year he began an ambitious project to make sense of vast changes that are currently transforming our trade.

In April last year, Gillmor announced to the readers of his weekly e-journal that he was going to write a book about the "new directions" journalism was taking.

Furthermore, he wanted to enlist the help of the online community and quickly set about publishing a rough outline inviting comments via e-mail. Gillmor said he wanted to know about what was missing from the draft, what was wrong, what needed more emphasis and what needed further investigation. He was inundated with replies.

In March this year, Gillmor went a step further and began releasing draft chapters of the forthcoming book online. It was a further invitation to communities of bloggers and enlightened journalists to scrutinise and annotate his work prior to the book's publication. Some wrote long, thoughtful passages about the nature of Gillmor's philosophical enquiry, others merely suggested tiny corrections or pointed out typos.

Each successive chapter was published, in weekly instalments, on a section of the *Mercury*'s website where Gillmor publishes his e-journal—more accurately described as a weblog or blog. This is a form of online diary that arranges postings in reverse chronological order and often interlinks with other blogs. In Gillmor's case, this means his readers can annotate his postings, correcting him if he is wrong or adding further detail to the story. His book formed an extension to this blogging technique.

Gillmor's draft chapters quickly began to attract a swarm of comments and a formal discussion group was formed at the foot of each. The majority of respondents were positive, but some were less sure. A few critics said his thesis amounts to a lot of hype, the net result, one said, of far too many "electronic whispers."

Others thought the blogging community he champions represents little more than a gaggle of wannabe political commentators. The internet being the internet, at least one wag recommended he keep his day job.

The net result—provisionally titled *Making the News: What Happens to Journalism and Society When Every Reader Can Be a Writer?*—will be published in July by O'Reilly & Associates, a company renowned for printing computer manuals. The book will be followed by a website featuring its own blog (naturally). It will be published under the Creative Commons licence, an alternative to the copyright notice that means anyone is free to copy, distribute or make derivative works as long as it is for non-commercial purposes.

But what exactly constitutes *Making the News*? As Gillmor writes in the (draft) introduction to the forthcoming book: "In the 20th century, making the news was almost entirely the province of journalists; the people we covered, or 'newsmakers'; and the legions of public relations and marketing people who manipulated everyone. The economics of publishing and broadcasting created large, arrogant institutions— call it Big Media, though even small-town newspapers and broadcasters exhibit some of the phenomenon's worst symptoms."

"The communication network itself will be a medium for everyone's voice."—Dan Gillmor, writer for the San Jose Mercury News

Gillmor is less precise on what will replace the arrogant institutions: "The lines will blur between producers and consumers, changing the role of both in ways we're only beginning to grasp. The communication network itself will be a medium for everyone's voice, not just the few who can afford to buy multimillion-dollar printing presses, launch satellites or win the government's permission to squat on the public's airwaves."

The central theme of the book is that "Big Media" has so far treated the news as a lecture. "We told you what the news was. You bought it, or you didn't. It was a world that bred complacency and arrogance on our part."

What Gillmor says is beginning to supplement—and in some cases replace—the "news as lecture" model is something more akin to a conversation or a seminar. Examples of this, often not-so-new kinds of media, can be found on any of the national newspaper talkboards or on the network of "Indymedia" sites or even on the shallow confines of talk radio.

Gillmor stresses that he has been doing the typical research— "reading, interviewing, thinking, organising, etc." Although he says he is still open to "anything major that we've missed," the book is now reaching its final stages. Gillmor was born in upstate New York before moving to Vermont, where he etched a living as a professional musician for nearly seven years. He says he fell into journalism "accidentally" after being asked to submit a music review to a local paper. He then worked for 15 years for newspapers in the mid-west before landing at the *Mercury* in 1994.

The *San Jose Mercury News* is a kind of local paper for Silicon Valley. Although it has, in US terms, a modest circulation of 280,000, (slightly more than *The Independent*) its influence spreads way beyond the San Francisco Bay area.

Nearly five years ago, Gillmor persuaded it to let him become the first mainstream journalist in the world to establish a blog. Its success helped to cement his reputation as one of the most respected technology journalists in the US and today the e-journal receives an average of 600,000 page views a month.

On the phone, Gillmor is quietly spoken and circumspect, his words coming slowly and forming neat, grammatically precise sentences. In contrast to many of the flamboyant stars of US technology journalism, Gillmor cuts a humble figure and this approach to journalism is also expressed in the book: "I take it for granted," he writes, "that my readers know more than I do—and this is a liberating, not threatening, fact of journalistic life."

Although his decision to focus on the American experience, "largely because journalism has flowered most widely in the nation whose founders explicitly recognised the essential role of the press," might rankle a few of us, the UK receives a couple of significant mentions. First, Gillmor cites the infamous McLibel trial in the mid-Nineties as being one of its earliest instances of "grassroots journalism." He argues that although the activists eventually lost part of the trial, it was the creation of the "path breaking" McSpotlight website (www.mcspotlight.org) and its "brilliant deconstruction of McDonald's marketing materials," that led to the burger giant taking "a beating in the court of public opinion." The site gave rise to the network of Indymedia sites that have grown around the anti-capitalism movement.

Gillmor also praises BBCi's recently launched iCan project: "What I like about it is the idea that a big journalism organisation is providing a tool to help people to become politically and socially active. Then watch what those people do and if it's new they report on it. In the end it may not work, but I believe that traditional media needs to experiment a lot more."

He also warns that the ability for new technology to democratise the media can cut two ways. Gillmor uses the recent instance of Bob Woodward and Dan Balz of *The Washington Post*'s interview with US Secretary of Defense Donald Rumsfeld. Immediately after the article's publication, the US Department of Defense posted a transcript of the interview on its DefenseLink website (www.defenselink.mil).

Gillmor uses this as an example to explain how old notions of journalists having the final say are beginning to unravel.

Although the English-speaking world dominates the book, for the most pronounced form of this new journalism, we have to look to South Korea. Three years ago, a crew of four people led by Oh Yeon-Ho launched the South Korean website Oh My News (www.ohmynews.com), a mix of straight news reporting and political commentary. Today, the site has a full-time staff of 53, including 35 reporters and editors. But it is its number of "citizen reporters" (a staggering 26,700 at last count) that gives it clout at grassroots level and made it the fifth most popular news source in the country. Oh My News has been widely credited with helping President Roh Moo-hyun win the popular vote at the last election.

But can this rise in amateur journalists be easily dismissed as just that? Not so. The bloggers are already competing with journalists and often pipping them to stories. But there is something else. Recently a prominent US blogger called Steve Gillard suggested that ordinary people adopt individual journalists to "fact-check, correct and otherwise provide them with the scrutiny they so sorely lack." The offer has been taken up by a few political activists but, for the moment at least, there are not enough willing bloggers to establish a system of man-to-man marking—but Gillard's suggestion is indicative of a much wider trend.

Diffusion, Use, and Effect of the Internet in China

By Jonathan J. H. Zhu and Enhai Wang
Communications of the ACM, April 2005

China has embraced the Internet. As of December 2004, 94 million people had gone online, making China the second largest Internet-user market in the world, behind only the U.S., according to the China Internet Network Information Center (CNNIC), which has carried out 15 semiannual surveys of Internet users in China since 1997.[1]

The growth trajectory of the country's Internet use appears to follow the common S-curve of technology adoption seen around the world (see Figure 1). The collapse of the worldwide Internet bubble in 2000 and 2001 slowed diffusion only momentarily. The rate of growth accelerated again in 2002 and 2003, driven by a few leading applications, including online chat, online games, and the Web-based short message service (SMS).

Internet use in China could have grown even more quickly. To help put things in perspective, it is worth comparing the growth of the Internet and the growth of the mobile phone market, both of which began in China in the early 1990s. While more costly than Internet access, mobile phones have become far more popular than using the Internet. As of December 2004, the country had more than 330 million mobile phone users, or 3.5 times more than the number of Internet users, according to the Ministry of Information Industry (www.mii.gov.cn). The implication is that wireless communication networks have had a greater effect transforming Chinese society than have wired information networks. Thus, the Internet's enormous potential remains largely unrealized but could change if the medium becomes as convenient and useful as mobile phones for Chinese users.

The evidence also suggests that the still relatively limited use of the Internet in China is not merely a function of resources. CNNIC surveys have repeatedly found that lack of computer skills is the number-one reason for not using the Internet, followed by lack of facilities, lack of time, and lack of interest. In addition, our multivariate analysis of survey data collected from Beijing and Guang-

---

1. The China Internet Netwok Information Center is the state designated agency for Internet usage statistics. Unless otherwise noted, all data reported here is based on its 1997–2004 survey (cnnic.com).

zhou from 2000 to 2002 also identified a series of psychological factors, including perceived usefulness, ease of use, and popularity, that effectively differentiate users from nonusers [9]. Money is not the main barrier.

As in many other developing countries, the digital divide has been a major concern in China. Defined as the difference in Internet adoption rates across the social segments of a society, the divide in China is most noticeable along educational and age dimensions [12]. For example, at the end of 2003, nearly half (49%) of those with college educations were using the Internet, compared to only 6% of those without college educations. Likewise, 23% of the young generation (18–34 years old) were using the Internet, compared to only 9% of the middle-aged (35–49) and only 3% of senior citizens (50 and older). In addition, geographic location also contributes to the divide, with the 10 most developed provinces, mostly along the east coast, having three times more Internet users than the 10 least developed provinces inland. Discounting these factors, Internet adoption rates are similar for men and women.

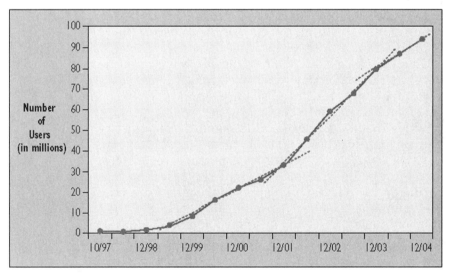

Figure 1. Diffusion of the Internet in China, 1997–2004; source: cnnic.cn.

Who Does What Online?

Based on our extensive tracking research on Internet usage behavior in China, the picture is fairly clear as to who is doing what online from what location, at what time, for how long, and for what purpose. Two out of three users in China go online from home, whereas the rest have access only at their workplaces, schools, or Internet cafés, which are widely available around the country and are particularly popular among millions of young migrant workers. In December 2004, a slight majority (56%) of Chinese users still relied on telephone dialup to connect to the Internet. Broadband connections have become increasingly popular, with 37% of users having it at home and 40% having it at their workplace/ school or Internet café. If Internet-adoption and access trends continue, we estimate that broadband will become the predominant method of connection at home by 2006 or sooner.

The average Chinese user spends about 13 hours per week (nearly two hours per day) online. Among users in major cities (such as Beijing in the north and Guangzhou in the south), going online has become the second most popular leisure activity, trailing only television viewing [9]. Internet use across China peaks during the evening hours (with 30%–50% of users logging on 7 P.M.–10 P.M.), conflicting with television's prime time. Online time is not equally distributed among users; instead, it is highly concentrated among a small group of enthusiastic users. For example, in Beijing and Guangzhou, 50% of these users (light users) account for only 12% of total online time; the other 50% (heavy users) take the other 82% of online time, with the most active 10% of the user population accounting for 40% of overall activity [9].

In contrast to the distinctive pattern of management information systems found in China [5], the country's use of the Internet is similar to that in most other countries. Since the first CNNIC survey in 1997, email has been China's most popular online activity. The average Chinese Internet user receives five legitimate messages per week, plus eight unwanted spam messages. They send out an average of four legitimate messages per week. Other popular online activities include (in order of descending popularity): using search engines; reading online news; browsing Web pages; peer-to-peer chat (via chat rooms or instant message tools); downloading software; group discussions (via bulletin board systems or forums); playing online games; using personal contact directories; and online entertainment (such as through MP3 and Flash). It appears the Internet is used firstly as an interpersonal communication medium (email and peer-to-peer and group interaction) and secondly as an information medium (search, news, browsing) (see Figure 2). Online entertainment (games, music, movies) has become increasingly popular but is still largely confined to the younger generation and is likely to remain in distant third place for some time.

The Internet is a global medium in terms of technological capability. But most Chinese users use it primarily as a domestic medium. For example, they spend over 80% of their time online on domestic Web sites and another 10% on overseas Web sites in the Chinese language. Only about 5% of their time online goes for non-Chinese overseas Web sites [9]. The locally oriented use of the Internet in China is not unique. For example, over 80% of online access in Taiwan, Japan, and Germany goes for locally produced Web sites.

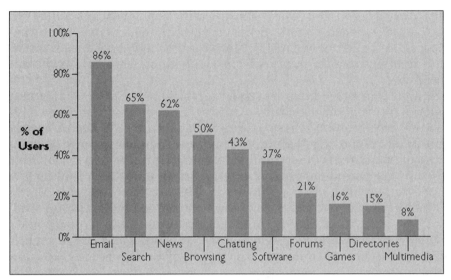

Figure 2. Top online activities among Chinese Internet users;
source: cnnic.cn

Societal Effect

As a medium used by nearly 100 million people, the Internet has
doubtless brought fundamental changes to Chinese society. A case
in point was the flow of information during the outbreak of SARS,
or Severe Acute Respiratory Syndrome, in 2003 [6]. For the first
five months, there was little coverage of the epidemic in the mainstream media. Tens of millions of Chinese residents learned about
it through phone calls, SMS messages, email, unofficial Web sites,
and other channels. In Guangdong province (where the epidemic
began) 40 million SMSs circulated daily. The first report the World
Health Organization received from China was an anonymous
email on February 20, 2003. After the central government began to
publicize the crisis, online traffic at eight national news Web sites
were reporting 20 million hits and 1,000 user-posted comments per
day. Sales of Web-based microphones and cameras took off, as people largely stayed home, shopping, conferencing, e-learning, and
peer-to-peer chatting online.

Despite ample anecdotal evidence, systematically evaluating the
Internet's effect has remained a challenge. Most studies have managed only simple comparisons of Internet users and nonusers.
While users and nonusers were indeed found to be remarkably different, the differences largely evaporated in more rigorous analy-
ses that took into account individual characteristics (such as age
and education), suggesting that the differences would have existed
even without the Internet. We found in our surveys of Beijing and
Guangzhou (2000–2002) that Internet users spend considerably
less time in face-to-face interactions with their families but more
time with friends (see Figure 3). However, these differences virtu-

ally disappeared, or were statistically nonsignificant, after we accounted for such factors as differences in age, gender, education, income, and marital status [4]. More convincingly, this null relationship holds in similar studies from Hong Kong, the U.S., and other societies [7].

Similar patterns have emerged in studies of the relationship among Internet use, cultural values [11], and civic efficacy [10], though exceptions to these findings exist. In a 2004 study on the quality of life among Beijing respondents, nonusers reported being happier than their heavy-Internet-using counterparts, even after discounting sociodemographic characteristics [1]. This finding was consistent with the often-cited 1995–1996 Carnegie-Mellon HomeNet study in the U.S. [3]. However, based on a follow-up study in 1998–1999, the Carnegie-Mellon team reported that "these negative effects are no longer evident," as "the Internet changed markedly, giving people much greater choice of contacts, activities, and information" [2].

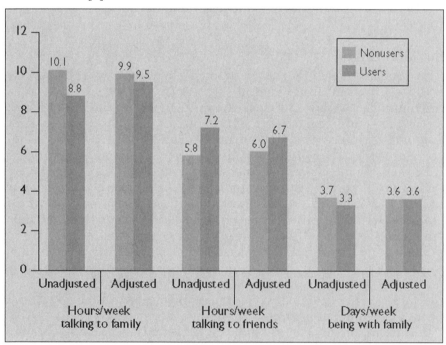

Figure 3. Socialization differences between users and nonusers; source: [5].

Conclusion

Our findings, along with those from CNNIC and other authoritative sources over the past eight years on the Internet in China are not only consistent with Internet research in most other countries, but with even earlier research on the effect of conventional mass media around the world. At the beginning of the 20th century, radio and television, along with other electronic media, were assumed by scholars, policy makers, and the general public to affect listeners and viewers instantaneously and invariantly. However, scientific research failed to prove the magic bullet power of the media, leading to the rise of limited-effects perspectives in the mid-20th century [8]. Only in the past 30 years, as media scholars looked into more subtle mechanisms (such as agenda-setting, cultivation, priming, and the spiral of silence, or how public opinion evolves from a silent majority into a true minority) over longer periods of time has the true nature of media influence begun to emerge. History seems to be repeating itself in China (and elsewhere), as research on the effect of the Internet struggles between the magic-bullet assumption of the new medium's power and the unconvincing empirical evidence.

The millions of people in China who use the Internet are changing the way the country's sophisticated urbanites communicate with one another and access and use information while creating appealing new entertainment options for tens of millions of young people. China's transformation into an online society is at an early stage, being limited in terms of both numbers of people online and how the network affects their lives. Moreover, the emerging evidence suggests that Chinese users may change their attitudes toward the Internet, as well as their lives more generally, as their experience with the new medium becomes more routine and pervasive.

References

1. Jin, J., Tan, X., and Xiong, C. On the interrelationship between media use and life quality (in Chinese). Paper presented at the Eighth National Communication Conference (Beijing, Oct. 22–24, 2004).

2. Kiesler, S., Kraut, R., Cummings, J., Boneva, B., Helgeson, V., and Crawford, A. Internet evolution and social impact. *IT & Society 1*, 1 (Summer 2002), 120–134; www.stanford.edu/group/siqss/itandsociety/ v01i01/v01i01a08.pdf.

3. Kraut, R., Lundmark, V., Patterson, M., Kiesler, S., Mukopadhyay, T., and Scherlis, W. Internet paradox: A social technology that reduces social involvement and psychological well-being? *American Psych. 53*, 9 (Sept. 1998), 1017–1031.

4. Lee, B. and Zhu, J. Internet use and sociability in mainland China and Hong Kong. *IT & Society 1*, 1 (Summer 2002), 219–237; www.stanford.edu/group/siqss/itandsociety/Vol01-1-A14-Lee-Zhu.pdf.

5. Martinsons, M.G. and Westwood, R. Management information systems in the Chinese business culture: An explanatory theory. *Inform. Mgt. 32*, 5 (Oct. 1997), 215–228.

6. Ming, D. The role of the Internet during the SARS crisis in China. Paper presented at the Fourth Asia-Pacific Symposium on Press and Scientific and Social Progress (Beijing, Nov. 17–18, 2004).

7. Robinson, J. and Nie, N. Introduction to IT and society, issue 1: Sociability. *IT & Society 1*, 1 (Summer 2002), i–xi; www.stanford.edu/group/siqss/itandsociety/v01i01/v01i01_intro.pdf.

8. Severin, W. and Tankard, J., Jr. *Communication Theories: Origins, Methods, and Uses in the Mass Media, 5th Ed.* Longman, New York, 2001.

9. Zhu, J. and He, Z. Perceived characteristics, perceived needs, and perceived popularity: Diffusion and use of the Internet in China. *Commun. Res. 29*, 4 (Aug. 2002), 466–495.

10. Zhu, J. and He, Z. Internet literacy and political efficacy in mainland China and Hong Kong. Paper presented at the International Symposium on Electronic Media, Markets, and Civil Society in Asia (Hong Kong, Apr. 2002).

11. Zhu, J. and He, Z. Information accessibility, user sophistication, and source credibility: The impact of the Internet on value orientations. *J. Comput.-Med. Commun. 7*, 2 (Jan. 2002); www.ascusc.org/jcmc/vol7/ issue2/china.html.

12. Zhu, J. Operational definition and preliminary test of the Digital Divide Index. In *Journalism and Communication Research in the 21st Century*, X. Wu, J. Wang, and A. Lin, Eds. Shantou University Press, Shantou, China, 2001, 203–211.

Growing Up Online

By Ana Veciana-Suarez
The Miami Herald, September 24, 2005

Growing up in Queens, N.Y., Antoinette Schreffler knew of one quick and easy way to keep in touch with her friends. She walked over to their houses.

Her daughter Samantha, a 13-year-old eighth-grader, wouldn't think of hoofing around her Coral Springs neighborhood. Instead, she heads over to the family computer and Instant Messages her buddies during online sessions that discuss everything from homework to boys to places they'll meet over the weekend—all in an abbreviated staccato language that rings foreign to most parents.

"It's fast and it's easy and I can talk to all my friends at once," explains Samantha of her predilection for IM. "It's like a big hang-out session."

Like Samantha, today's youngsters are relying more on new methods of communication and less on traditional sources to talk with friends, to do homework, to plan their outings, to stay in touch with parents, and to keep tabs on pals who live crosstown or cross-country. Cell phones, IM, text messaging, e-mail, iPods, video games—all have changed the way teens, particularly middle schoolers, socialize.

No longer dependent on their parents to take them places, teens roam the Internet with freedom and facility. "It has given them a lot more mobility than their parents ever had," says Frances Jacobson Harris, author of *I Found It on the Internet: Coming of Age Online*. "They can be together and get together without leaving the house, and many times they can operate under the parental radar."

This kind of access means they're doing the business of growing up—figuring out who they are and how they relate to the larger community—online. Yes, the transition to young adulthood is still the same, but now they hide from parents, declare their crushes and establish a social hierarchy without physical contact. Technology has enabled them to rewrite the rules on privacy and shed the sometimes shy awkwardness of adolescence for bolder online personalities.

Be Yourself Online

Says Jessica Cleveland, a Broward County eighth-grader who spends about two hours a day on the computer: "Online you can be more yourself because you're not so conscious. You don't have to worry about how you look or how you sound. It doesn't matter if you just woke up and have bags under your eyes."

In the ever-changing world that youngsters tap and dial into, IM reigns supreme because of its accessibility. "I can't hang out in the mall by myself because my mother won't let me, but I can IM," says Gabriela Gross, a sixth-grader at Highland Oaks Middle School. "All my friends are on and I can do a chat with 10 people all at once if I want to."

And while technology affords teens an independence they didn't have a generation ago, it also gives them an early entry into the adult world—both the good and the bad. Seventy-six percent of teens get their news online, a whopping increase from the 38 percent who did so in 2000, according to a study by the Pew Internet & American Life Project. They also surf the net to obtain health information (31 percent) and make purchases (43 percent).

"I can't hang out in the mall by myself because my mother won't let me, but I can IM."—Gabriela Gross, a sixth-grader

---

But for all its magic, technology can be a double-edged sword. Experts say some kids spend too much time in front of a screen, whether it's a television set, a computer or a cell phone. And parents worry that this brave new world hosts dangers they cannot control.

On Alert

"You have to be constantly going in there and asking, 'Who are you talking to? What websites are you on?'" says Maria Gross, mother of 12-year-old fraternal twins. "They know much more about it than I do."

Many teens report pop-up ads for inappropriate material and admit to visiting websites their parents would probably not approve of.

"What I've found is that teens are much more sexually aware even if they're not experienced," says Sylvia Rimm, of studies she conducted for her book, *Growing Up Too Fast: The Rimm Report on the Secret World of America's Middle Schoolers.* "They have access to more [than their parents did]."

The popularity of IMing is a prime example of the demand for speed and easy accessibility. It has become wildly popular, more so even than cell phones, simply because cellular use—often with minutes shared in a family plan—costs money and can be restricted more easily by a parent.

IM, in fact, seems to have overtaken e-mail as the preferred mode of communication with this set because it happens instantly and it's free. E-mail, kids say, is for serious subjects, for a formal letter, or for longer explanations to a large number of people. It is what you might use with a grown-up.

"E-mail takes too long," explains Dominique Mortimer, a seventh-grader from Richmond Heights. "And you don't hear back right away, either. I love IM and text messaging because it's fast. Old people are just getting used to e-mail now. I use e-mail for teachers and IM for friends."

Amanda Lenhart, senior research specialist for the Pew Internet & American Life Project, explains the popularity this way: "IM feels more like a conversation. It's quick exchanges back and forth."

Staying Connected

Even when teens aren't close to a computer, they can post an away message—a quote, a poem, an inside joke—that still keeps them connected to friends in the virtual world.

Whether IMing or e-mailing, this virtual world often emboldens even the shiest of teens.

Whether IMing or e-mailing, this virtual world often emboldens even the shiest of teens. They will tell each other things that might be too embarrassing to say on the phone or in person.

Cleveland, the eighth-grader at Olsen Middle School in Dania Beach, says she knows of girls who have dumped their boyfriends online "because it's easier and it doesn't make you feel so guilty." Some kids also use it to ask someone out on a date or to confess their latest crushes.

But the bullying and bickering common to that age group, particularly among girls, doesn't stop at the school cafeteria. Technology—blocking a buddy from your IM chat—can be used to exclude others, too. And online jargon becomes a way of establishing credibility. Use the wrong language style and you'll reveal your cluelessness.

This instantaneous and uninhibited communication also is rewriting the rules on privacy, and it worries some experts. A generation ago, secrets were usually told one on one. "Now everything is out in the open and though they might have a special screen name, their friends know exactly who they are," Rimm says.

It's not uncommon, she adds, for youngsters to share information that was once considered private: "They might write about what's happening at the moment without thinking or censoring themselves. They'll tell everybody that mom and dad are fighting and that they're worried they might get divorced.

Along with Instant Messaging, other forms of mobile technology are gaining in popularity—primarily cell phones. Cell ownership among 12 to 14 year olds increased from 13 percent in February 2002 to 40 percent by the end of 2004, according to a study by NOP World Technology. Many young cell users love the camera phones and the text messaging options that come with the newer models but complain that they can't use them as freely as other technology.

Private Line

Dominique has had a cell phone since she was in second grade. Her newest model not only text-messages and takes photos, but it also accepts e-mails.

"It's like my own private line," she says. "I feel naked without it."

Cell phone use, however, tends to differ among the sexes. While girls use it as a communication source, boys are entranced by the technology itself. In fact, they play online and sometimes organize their social calendar around the issue of a new version of a favorite game.

Gabriela Gross loves to chat with her friends on the phone, for instance, but twin brother Michael likes the games he can play on it. He says a cell is more of a want than a need in a young teen's life.

"Cell phones are good because you can call your mom to pick you up, but most of my friends are like me. We'd rather play games," he says.

It's Got a Hold on You

By Douglas Rushkoff
WWW.RUSHKOFF.COM, May 26, 2005

The mobile phones in our hands may have a more totemic role in our lives than we suspect.

There's something magical about the objects we use every day. No, not that plastic pen, but the one over there in the holder on your desk, the Mont Blanc. Or the wallet in your pocket, actually a bit too worn out, but a gift from your daughter. Or the portable clock radio you saved when going through your dad's stuff after he died.

Willie Nelson has his favorite guitar, so beat up it has holes in the front. Jack Nicklaus had his favorite putter, not that its exact weight and dimensions couldn't be reproduced. Philip K. Dick had a favorite typewriter, on which he wrote nearly all his stories.

We form emotional, almost spiritual attachments to the objects in our lives. Occultists would tell us that, through projection, we have "charged up" these things with psychic energy, and this is what gives them their power. The rabbit's foot or rosary beads don't come off the shelf at the trinkets shop with any special power, but the continued association of those objects with one's prayers or desires, the way one touches them as a constant reminder of his or her intentions, generates an energy of expectation all its own.

Does the same thing happen between people and their cell phones? And if it does, is this level of object infatuation a good thing for the industry, or an obstacle to selling more phones?

Clearly, now that mobile phones have been incorporated into the most personal moments and pockets in our lives, they have become our intimate partners. They hold the photos of our families, the ringtones sampled from our favorite songs, and the wallpaper that mirrors our aesthetic. Whether or not we put a Hello Kitty sticker on our clamshells, our handsets take on totemic value both as reflections of who we are, and expressions of what we are striving yet to be.

Beyond that, like the conch shells held up to the ear that seemed to tell our ancestors their history and futures, cell phones are handheld objects that often hold news of our fate, from the voice-mails of potential sex partners to the SMS stock quotes of our latest investments. So many of our hopes and fears are broadcast to us through (or is it from?) the six-ounce rectangle in our breast pocket. On an anthropological level, we humans can't help but relate to their immense power with a bit of fear, reverence and mystery.

Maybe this explains why people in China have been lining up to get their mobile phones blessed by Buddhist monks. According to Intel ethnographer Genevieve Bell, who observed the phenomenon, it is the size and physicality of cell phones, like the weight of a pocket Bible or the portability of rosary beads, that makes us feel comfortable investing them with spiritual value. Bell feels that these blessings could be a way to "neutralize and naturalize the technology."

But elsewhere in China, for a superstitious man who bid 9 million yuan ($1.1 million) for a lucky cell phone number, the spiritual (and financial) significance is far from neutral. Apparently the number— 135 8585 8585—which has a similar pronunciation in Chinese to "let me be rich be rich be rich be rich." So, unlike a number that's a birthdate or simply easy to remember, it's as if each time this guy's number is dialed, a mantra is repeated, and a spell is being cast on his behalf.

This seems more advanced than simply "naturalizing" technology, as Bell suggests. It's the wholesale appropriation of technology for spiritual and magical purposes. Moreover, here in societies already inundated with wireless technologies, this sort of spiritual repurposing has become ubiquitous.

In most cases, the phone itself is transparent, and the application or content takes on spiritual dimensions. Stephen Goddard, co-editor of ShipofFools.com, has been tracking products targeting the "born-again buck." Apart from conventional religious paraphernalia, the devoted can purchase popular hymns as ringtones and phone cover crucifixes with holographic images of Jesus, or sign up for daily SMS messages from the Pope.

Meanwhile, Muslims can use the Ilkone i-800 mobile phone to access an Islamic calendar, a Mecca direction-finder, a searchable version of the Koran, prayer times, alarms and an authentic Azaan (call to prayer) voice. And New Agers can register through The Mobile Deepak Chopra website to sign receive "enlightening quotes, inspirational images, success tips and a weekly message from Deepak himself, combined in a mobile application that inspires, motivates and provides understanding of the Laws in a simple, easy-to-use format."

My guess is that users' desire to relate to their handheld wireless technology in spiritual and magical ways will only increase. But this may happen in different ways in different places. Cultures where this technology is new, such as those visited by Bell, relate to the phone object in a magical way, but are just beginning to develop a spiritual sensibility about the software and applications they use. Cultures where phones are already integrated into the fabric of life, however, already use a wide array of spiritual applications, but are just beginning to develop a sense of totemic connection to the cell phones, themselves. Of course, the more valuable people perceive their individual cell phones to be, the less likely they may be to trade up for new ones. Still, for savvy manufacturers and operators, there's still plenty of room to build on these growing trends.

For instance take a culture where hi-tech and hi-totem already coexist, like Taiwan, where in an effort to differentiate its brand, manufacturer Okwap released a divinely blessed limited-edition cellphone. In addition to being blessed in her temple, the phones have wallpapers, ringtones and holograms all based on Matsu, the popular Chinese goddess of the sea.

Although I usually come down hard against such tactics as exploitative or degrading of people's beliefs, I'm finding it hard to feel too terrible about gods, goddesses and other mystical traditions being incorporated into phones as a form of brand differentiation. In a sense, integrating them all with each other only underscores what a central role traditions, technologies and target marketing now play in our lives, and forces us to make a more conscious choice about what we believe in, and why.

II. New Media and the Written Word

Editor's Introduction

In his article "Bad News," Richard A. Posner of the *New York Times* declares, "The conventional news media are embattled. Attacked by both left and right in book after book, rocked by scandals, challenged by upstart bloggers, they have become a focus of controversy and concern." "[Bloggers] are your Nemesis in the making," Phil Boas writes to his fellow journalists in *Masthead*. "Lovers of traditional literature—the stuff squashed between stiff or flimsy covers, arranged in clumps of typography and that remains as unassailable as stone tablets bearing sacred hieroglyphics—ought to be afraid," asserts Julia Keller in the *Chicago Tribune*, while discussing the effect of the new methods of circulating literary texts enabled by the Internet. Though these inflammatory statements should be treated with some degree of skepticism, they nevertheless reveal the turbulent nature of publishing today. The industry is undergoing a period of rapid change, as large firms are forced to adjust to a market in which individuals can publish material and attract an audience with little financial expenditure. This section, "New Media and the Written Word," explores this trend, focusing on news and book publishers.

The chapter opens with Patrick Beeson's "The Ethical Dilemma of Blogging in the Media," which examines the state of the blogosphere and the efforts by some to establish a code of ethics for it. Those working toward this goal have been modeling their prospective code on the one followed by journalists. Beeson discusses the debate among those who propose that bloggers maintain a standard as rigorous as mainstream journalists, those who oppose codifying a set of rules, and those who occupy the middle ground, arguing that some standard of honesty and transparency ought to govern the blogosphere but acknowledging that the nature of the medium will likely thwart any attempt to establish a general standard.

Posner takes us from the blogosphere to the newsroom with a discussion of the current state of journalism in "Bad News." He reviews the newspaper culture and reflects on how and why it is changing. Bloggers present, Posner states, perhaps the gravest "challenge to the journalistic establishment"—but not just because they are competing with traditional journalists: The larger problem is that bloggers are not, for a variety of reasons, held to the same standards that journalists are and thus do not need to be as careful or as conscientious when breaking a story. Nor are bloggers constrained by the commercial realities of news outlets. They can, for example, follow a story for much longer than regular reporters, who have to move on to new scoops for fear of losing their audience. Interestingly, another major threat the blogosphere poses to the mainstream press is that it "has a better error-correction machinery than the conventional media do. The rapidity with which vast masses of information are pooled and sifted leaves the conventional media in the dust," a fact which has led some reporters to rush their work, creating more potential for error and undermining the quality of the news as a whole.

Boas's "Bloggers: The Light at the End of the Newspaper's Tunnel" and Michael J. Korzi's "The Benefits of Blogs" examine the relationship between bloggers and journalists from a slightly more positive angle. Boas, while acknowledging the adversarial relationship between the mainstream media and the blogosphere, argues that the conflict will be good for news journalism in general. After all, the blogosphere feeds off the traditional news, taking up its stories and "creating stimulating and often irresistible discussion around the news we produce. Journalism tomorrow, thanks to forces like the blogosphere, will grow more competitive." Korzi considers the debate from a similar perspective. In detailing both the negative and positive qualities of bloggers, he finds their contribution to journalism is "largely positive." Ted Landphair in "Are Bloggers Journalists?" arrives at a similar conclusion, asserting that mainstream journalists should welcome bloggers.

Having focused on the news media thus far, the chapter shifts to book publishing, an industry that has been less threatened by Internet-based media, for books, while available online, do not lend themselves to the online reading experience as easily as newspaper and magazine articles do. Keller's "Plugged-in Proust: Has E-lit Come of Age?" finds the potential for literature on the Web is growing as the e-book carves out a niche for itself. A case is also made for the value of blogs, e-mails, text messages, and other technology-generated genres as literary texts. In the end, William J. Mitchell, who heads the Media Arts and Sciences program at the Massachusetts Institute of Technology (MIT), maintains, "All of these new formats just enrich and democratize literature." The section concludes, however, on a different note. In "Who Will Have the Last Word on Digital Frontier?" Mandy Garner reports on the posting of electronic, sometimes searchable, versions of already published books online by numerous companies, including Amazon, Random House, and Google. The consequences of this development are yet to be clear, but the debate over it has already proved thought-provoking.

The Ethical Dilemma of Blogging in the Media

By Patrick Beeson
QUILL, April 2005

Bloggers are a rough-and-tumble lot. They are the publishing cowboys of the media frontier. And like the untamed West, the blogosphere is full of mavericks who fail to think before they write.

Even worse is that some of these cowboys refuse to adhere to a set of ethical rules.

But this could change, as many notable bloggers push for a code ethics. Like town pastors, these bloggers are preaching the virtue and benefit of being honest, truthful and transparent with readers.

Unfortunately, this approach doesn't seem to sit well with a largely nonprofessional lot that began writing as a means to vent dissatisfaction with traditional media.

"Codes are good in articulating the principles that guide us, principles that give us moral compass and moral gyroscope for our behavior," said Bob Steele, director of the Poynter Institute's ethics program. "Professional codes set the boundaries, but they are not the end all, be all."

Steele co-authored the paper "Earn your own trust, roll your own ethics: Transparency and beyond" with Bill Mitchell, Poynter director of publishing and online editor. The two created the piece for a blogging conference at Harvard. Steele said bloggers and journalists share a common aim with ethics—credibility with their audiences. He said a blogger's credibility is built on a number of ethical values, which can be shaped by the individual blogger.

"This forces us to grapple in the gray area, rather than accept absolutes," Steele said.

It's also about respect.

"There's an obligation for fairness to others in any circumstance in which we're writing," he said. "We should not be disrespectful in how we go about that expression.

"Disrespect erodes relationships . . . it's anti-ethical to the spirit of blogging."

Code or No Code?

It's what these ethical values are that is generating controversy with bloggers, including longtime blogger Rebecca Blood. Her blog "Rebecca's Pocket" has archives dating to the early days of blogging in April 1999. She devoted an entire chapter of her 2002 book "The Weblog handbook: Practical advise on creating and maintaining your blog" to blogging ethics.

Blood disagrees with a formalized code of ethics for bloggers, such as that proposed by Jonathan Dube, MSNBC.com Managing Producer and Publisher of Cyberjournalist.net. Instead, she includes in her book a list of ethical standards for non-journalist bloggers.

"I think it's unrealistic for the blogger to uphold journalistic standards," she said. "Most of us aren't interested in being a journalist."

But for those who are, Blood said it's reasonable to expect them to be transparent with sources, biases and behavior. She said bloggers must also be willing to publish corrections, which are "never as much fun."

> *"I think it's unrealistic for the blogger to uphold journalistic standards."*
> —Rebecca Blood, a blogger

Dube's "Blogger's Code of Ethics"—posted on the media convergence and technology Web site Cyberjournalist.net—was created by modifying the Society of Professional Journalists Code of Ethics for the blogosphere.

"Responsible bloggers should recognize that they are publishing words publicly, and therefore have certain ethical obligations to their readers, the people they write about and society in general," Dube writes in the Code's preface. He also suggests bloggers choose their own best practices and use his code as a guideline.

Blood and Dube's differing ideas intertwine in thought but have split backing from media critics.

J. D. Lasica, a former *Sacramento Bee* editor and supporter of grass-roots media, said he agrees with Blood. He said bloggers sometimes act as journalists, but not always. But in those instances, he believes they should be held to a stricter standard.

"I think an 'ethics code' is something that bloggers will never accept," he said. "While journalism has decades of tradition as a craft, during which certain norms and practices came into being before being codified into a code, blogs aren't at that point yet."

However, Lasica does believe certain customs and norms are beginning to emerge: transparency, passionate blogging, honesty, trust in readers and integrity in one's reputation. He said for bloggers to "write the truth" is always the most difficult ethical imperative to follow.

Lasica said bloggers are more honest than news organizations in admitting when they're wrong. He said they also are more forthcoming about biases and motives.

"Being honest and truthful—and writing with your readers uppermost in mind—should be the aim of every blogger and journalist," Lasica said.

Ethics from the Mainstream

Blood said another ethical situation bloggers must recognize is the difference between being popular and being credible.

"It's the tabloid factor," she said. "Just because it's in print, doesn't mean it's accurate. You can't always judge the accuracy of any medium by the size of its audience."

However, *The New York Times* has a huge audience, and it's starting to embrace blogging—with tender steps.

"We have not had any ethical problems with blogs, but our experience has been pretty modest," said Len Apcar, editor in chief of NYTimes.com.

The NYTimes.com blogging exploits began in 2003 with op-ed columnist Nick Kristof's "Kristof Responds." That was followed by the more ambitious "Times on the Trail" news blog that chronicled the recent presidential race. There have been other blogs for special news events written by staff writers.

Apcar said he is more concerned with bloggers' credibility, independence and the reliability of information on the Internet, than whether those bloggers are journalists.

"I would rather not see the Web overcome with rumors, half-truths and falsehoods," he said.

To do this, Apcar said bloggers should be free of commercial or partisan interests, and should dispense information and opinion that is not influenced by any outside force. He hopes the recent revelations of bloggers' taking payments for voicing a particular point of view, such as former Howard Dean staffer Zephyr Teachout's report that the campaign had paid two bloggers for their positive praise, will not continue.

"I think bloggers or journalists taking money for promoting a point of view is a reckless practice and poisonous to the credibility of journalism in any form," he said.

In fact, Apcar believes credibility is the most important asset anyone in the media has.

Sheila Lennon, features and interactive producer for the *Providence Journal* as well as its resident blogger, said blogging in the newsroom doesn't involve different ethical concerns.

"I could theoretically announce some company policy on my blog before it was implemented," she said, "but I'm not that stupid."

Lennon said some newsroom habits that are also effective in blogging include: working for readers, checking the small things, posting corrections in all instances and using words such as "says" and "said" rather than colorful words for quotes.

"I think a lot of the bias in political blogs comes from little word choices such as these," she said.

Transparency Equals Credibility

Nearly all media critics and bloggers agree that transparency can lead to credibility.

Kelly McBride, ethics group leader at the Poynter Institute, said transparency in journalism means the reader or viewer can tell how a reporter got his or her information. She said blogs are sporadic in their use of transparency, with some very transparent and others not at all.

"Yes, I believe it (transparency) goes hand in hand with ethical decision making," she said. "But it's not the end all and be all.

"Ethics is much bigger than transparency."

McBride said because transparency can't be enforced with bloggers, it's only an issue if they are concerned with their independence and credibility.

"It's not an issue for the bloggers who really don't care about those principles," she said. "If you are a reader looking for transparency, blogs will let you down."

Mitchell and Steele's ethics paper contends that a bloggers' disclosure in the areas of principles, processes and the personal, can help one move beyond transparency to accountability.

Nearly all media critics and bloggers agree that transparency can lead to credibility.

Steele said he champions the concept of transparency for everyone practicing some form of journalism, including bloggers.

"It's valuable because it gives insight into why certain decisions are being made," he said. "It helps readers understand a bit of the (journalism) process, and that's good."

Steele said transparency builds trust with readers, which could help create credibility. But he said it cannot be used independent of ethics.

"Transparency (by itself) is not enough," Steele said. "You can be transparent, but unethical."

Mitchell agrees. He said blogs must be transparent because they continue to be much more personal than mainstream media. Mitchell also said the personalized nature of blogs means bloggers' faithfulness to ethics is determined on a more fundamental, moral level.

"If you have an intent in being a moral human being, there are issues at stake far more basic than journalism or blogging," he said.

Mitchell said it's this moral awareness that must be part of a bloggers' adherence to the concept of transparency if they are to be ethical.

"The core issue is that when you publish something, that (action) carries responsibility," he said. "There is an ethical responsibility whether you're with an organization, or whether you're standing on that soapbox in a blogging town square."

Bad News

By Richard A. Posner
The New York Times, July 31, 2005

The conventional news media are embattled. Attacked by both left and right in book after book, rocked by scandals, challenged by upstart bloggers, they have become a focus of controversy and concern. Their audience is in decline, their credibility with the public in shreds. In a recent poll conducted by the Annenberg Public Policy Center, 65 percent of the respondents thought that most news organizations, if they discover they've made a mistake, try to ignore it or cover it up, and 79 percent opined that a media company would hesitate to carry negative stories about a corporation from which it received substantial advertising revenues.

The industry's critics agree that the function of the news is to inform people about social, political, cultural, ethical and economic issues so that they can vote and otherwise express themselves as responsible citizens. They agree on the related point that journalism is a profession rather than just a trade and therefore that journalists and their employers must not allow profit considerations to dominate, but must acknowledge an ethical duty to report the news accurately, soberly, without bias, reserving the expression of political preferences for the editorial page and its radio and television counterparts. The critics further agree, as they must, that 30 years ago news reporting was dominated by newspapers and by television network news and that the audiences for these media have declined with the rise of competing sources, notably cable television and the Web.

The audience decline is potentially fatal for newspapers. Not only has their daily readership dropped from 52.6 percent of adults in 1990 to 37.5 percent in 2000, but the drop is much steeper in the 20-to-49-year-old cohort, a generation that is, and as it ages will remain, much more comfortable with electronic media in general and the Web in particular than the current elderly are.

At this point the diagnosis splits along political lines. Liberals, including most journalists (because most journalists are liberals), believe that the decline of the formerly dominant "mainstream" media has caused a deterioration in quality. They attribute this decline to the rise of irresponsible journalism on the right, typified by the Fox News Channel (the most-watched cable television news channel), Rush Limbaugh's radio talk show and right-wing blogs by Matt Drudge and others. But they do not spare the mainstream media, which, they contend, provide in the name of balance an echo chamber for the right. To these critics, the deterioration of journalism is exemplified by the attack of the "Swift boat" Vietnam veterans on Senator John Kerry during the 2004 election campaign. The critics describe the attack as consisting of lies propagated by the new right-wing media and reported as news by mainstream media made supine by anxiety over their declining fortunes.

Critics on the right applaud the rise of the conservative media as a long-overdue corrective to the liberal bias of the mainstream media, which, according to Jim A. Kuypers, the author of "Press Bias and Politics," are "a partisan collective which both consciously and unconsciously attempts to persuade the public to accept its interpretation of the world as true." Fourteen percent of Americans describe themselves as liberals, and 26 percent as conservatives. The corresponding figures for journalists are 56 percent and 18 percent. This means that of all journalists who consider themselves either liberal or conservative, 76 percent consider themselves liberal, compared with only 35 percent of the public that has a stated political position.

The rise of new media, itself mainly an economic rather than a political phenomenon, has caused polarization, pushing the already liberal media farther left.

So politically one-sided are the mainstream media, the right complains (while sliding over the fact that the owners and executives, as distinct from the working journalists, tend to be far less liberal), that not only do they slant the news in a liberal direction; they will stop at nothing to defeat conservative politicians and causes. The right points to the "60 Minutes II" broadcast in which Dan Rather paraded what were probably forged documents concerning George W. Bush's National Guard service, and to *Newsweek*'s erroneous report, based on a single anonymous source, that an American interrogator had flushed a copy of the Koran down the toilet (a physical impossibility, one would have thought).

Strip these critiques of their indignation, treat them as descriptions rather than as denunciations, and one sees that they are consistent with one another and basically correct. The mainstream media are predominantly liberal—in fact, more liberal than they used to be. But not because the politics of journalists have changed. Rather, because the rise of new media, itself mainly an economic rather than a political phenomenon, has caused polarization, pushing the already liberal media farther left.

The news media have also become more sensational, more prone to scandal and possibly less accurate. But note the tension between sensationalism and polarization: the trial of Michael Jackson got tremendous coverage, displacing a lot of political coverage, but it had no political valence.

The interesting questions are, first, the why of these trends, and, second, so what?

The why is the vertiginous decline in the cost of electronic communication and the relaxation of regulatory barriers to entry, leading to the proliferation of consumer choices. Thirty years ago the average number of television channels that Americans could receive was seven; today, with the rise of cable and satellite television, it is 71. Thirty years ago there was no Internet, therefore no Web, hence no online newspapers and magazines, no blogs. The public's consumption of news and opinion used to be like sucking on a straw; now it's like being sprayed by a fire hose.

To see what difference the elimination of a communications bottleneck can make, consider a town that before the advent of television or even radio had just two newspapers because economies of scale made it impossible for a newspaper with a small circulation to break even. Each of the two, to increase its advertising revenues, would try to maximize circulation by pitching its news to the median reader, for that reader would not be attracted to a newspaper that flaunted extreme political views. There would be the same tendency to political convergence that is characteristic of two-party political systems, and for the same reason—attracting the least committed is the key to obtaining a majority.

One of the two newspapers would probably be liberal and have a loyal readership of liberal readers, and the other conservative and have a loyal conservative readership. That would leave a middle range. To snag readers in that range, the liberal newspaper could not afford to be too liberal or the conservative one too conservative. The former would strive to be just liberal enough to hold its liberal readers, and the latter just conservative enough to hold its conservative readers. If either moved too close to its political extreme, it would lose readers in the middle without gaining readers from the extreme, since it had them already.

But suppose cost conditions change, enabling a newspaper to break even with many fewer readers than before. Now the liberal newspaper has to worry that any temporizing of its message in an effort to attract moderates may cause it to lose its most liberal readers to a new, more liberal newspaper; for with small-scale entry into the market now economical, the incumbents no longer have a secure base. So the liberal newspaper will tend to become even more liberal and, by the same process, the conservative newspaper more conservative. (If economies of scale increase, and as a result the number of newspapers grows, the opposite ideological change will be observed, as happened in the 19th century. The introduction of the "penny press" in the 1830's enabled newspapers to obtain large circulations and thus finance themselves by selling advertising; no longer did they have to depend on political patronage.)

The current tendency to political polarization in news reporting is thus a consequence of changes not in underlying political opinions but in costs, specifically the falling costs of new entrants. The rise of the conservative Fox News Channel caused CNN to shift to the left. CNN was going to lose many of its conservative viewers to Fox anyway, so it made sense to increase its appeal to its remaining viewers by catering more assiduously to their political preferences.

The tendency to greater sensationalism in reporting is a parallel phenomenon. The more news sources there are, the more intense the struggle for an audience. One tactic is to occupy an overlooked niche—peeling away from the broad-based media a segment of the consuming public whose interests were not catered to previously. That is the tactic that produces polarization. Another is to "shout louder" than the competitors, where shouting takes the form of a sensational, attention-grabbing discovery, accusation, claim or photograph. According to James T. Hamilton in his valuable book "All the News That's Fit to Sell," this even explains why the salaries paid news anchors have soared: the more competition there is for an audience, the more valuable is a celebrity newscaster.

The argument that competition increases polarization assumes that liberals want to read liberal newspapers and conservatives conservative ones. Natural as that assumption is, it conflicts with one of the points on which left and right agree—that people consume news and opinion in order to become well informed about public issues. Were this true, liberals would read conservative newspapers, and conservatives liberal newspapers, just as scientists test their hypotheses by confronting them with data that may refute them. But that is not how ordinary people (or, for that matter, scientists) approach political and social issues. The issues are too numerous, uncertain and complex, and the benefit to an individual of becoming well informed about them too slight, to invite sustained, disinterested attention. Moreover, people don't like being in a state of doubt, so they look for information that will support rather than undermine their existing beliefs. They're also uncomfortable seeing their beliefs challenged on issues that are bound up with their economic welfare, physical safety or religious and moral views.

So why do people consume news and opinion? In part it is to learn of facts that bear directly and immediately on their lives—hence the greater attention paid to local than to national and international news. They also want to be entertained, and they find scandals, violence, crime, the foibles of celebrities and the antics of the powerful all mightily entertaining. And they want to be confirmed in their beliefs by seeing them echoed and elaborated by more articulate, authoritative and prestigious voices. So they accept, and many relish, a partisan press. Forty-three percent of the respondents in the poll by the Annenberg Public Policy Center thought it "a good thing if some news organizations have a decidedly political point of view in their coverage of the news."

Being profit-driven, the media respond to the actual demands of their audience rather than to the idealized "thirst for knowledge" demand posited by public intellectuals and deans of journalism schools. They serve up what the consumer wants, and the more intense the competitive pressure, the better they do it. We see this in the media's coverage of political campaigns. Relatively little attention is paid to issues. Fundamental questions, like the actual difference in policies that might result if one candidate rather than the other won, get little play. The focus instead is on who's ahead, viewed as a function of campaign tactics, which are meticulously reported. Candidates' statements are evaluated not for their truth but for their adroitness; it is assumed, without a hint of embarrassment, that a political candidate who levels with voters disqualifies himself from being taken seriously, like a racehorse that tries to hug the outside of the track. News coverage of a political campaign is oriented to a public that enjoys competitive sports, not to one that is civic-minded.

News coverage of a political campaign is oriented to a public that enjoys competitive sports, not to one that is civic-minded.

We saw this in the coverage of the selection of Justice Sandra Day O'Connor's successor. It was played as an election campaign; one article even described the jockeying for the nomination by President Bush as the "primary election" and the fight to get the nominee confirmed by the Senate the "general election" campaign. With only a few exceptions, no attention was paid to the ability of the people being considered for the job or the actual consequences that the appointment was likely to have for the nation.

Does this mean that the news media were better before competition polarized them? Not at all. A market gives people what they want, whether they want the same thing or different things. Challenging areas of social consensus, however dumb or even vicious the consensus, is largely off limits for the media, because it wins no friends among the general public. The mainstream media do not kick sacred cows like religion and patriotism.

Not that the media lie about the news they report; in fact, they have strong incentives not to lie. Instead, there is selection, slanting, decisions as to how much or how little prominence to give a particular news item. Giving a liberal spin to equivocal economic data when conservatives are in power is, as the Harvard economists Sendhil Mullainathan and Andrei Shleifer point out, a matter of describing the glass as half empty when conservatives would describe it as half full.

Journalists are reluctant to confess to pandering to their customers' biases; it challenges their self-image as servants of the general interest, unsullied by commerce. They want to think they inform the public, rather than just satisfying a consumer demand no more elevated or consequential than the demand for cosmetic surgery in Brazil or bullfights in Spain. They believe in "deliberative democracy"—democracy as the system in which the people determine policy through deliberation on the issues. In his preface to "The Future of Media" (a collection of articles edited by Robert W. McChesney, Russell Newman and Ben Scott), Bill Moyers writes that "democracy can't exist without an informed public." If this is true, the United States is not a democracy (which may be Moyers's dyspeptic view). Only members of the intelligentsia, a tiny slice of the population, deliberate on public issues.

> *The public's interest in factual accuracy is less an interest in truth than a delight in the unmasking of the opposition's errors.*

The public's interest in factual accuracy is less an interest in truth than a delight in the unmasking of the opposition's errors. Conservatives were unembarrassed by the errors of the Swift Boat veterans, while taking gleeful satisfaction in the exposure of the forgeries on which Dan Rather had apparently relied, and in his resulting fall from grace. They reveled in *Newsweek*'s retracting its story about flushing the Koran down a toilet yet would prefer that American abuse of prisoners be concealed. Still, because there is a market demand for correcting the errors and ferreting out the misdeeds of one's enemies, the media exercise an important oversight function, creating accountability and deterring wrongdoing. That, rather than educating the public about the deep issues, is their great social mission. It shows how a market produces a social good as an unintended byproduct of self-interested behavior.

The limited consumer interest in the truth is the key to understanding why both left and right can plausibly denounce the same media for being biased in favor of the other. Journalists are writing to meet a consumer demand that is not a demand for uncomfortable truths. So a newspaper that appeals to liberal readers will avoid exposés of bad behavior by blacks or homosexuals, as William McGowan charges in "Coloring the News"; similarly, Daniel Okrent, the first ombudsman of *The New York Times*, said that the news pages of *The Times* "present the social and cultural aspects of same-sex marriage in a tone that approaches cheerleading." Not only would such exposés offend liberal readers who are not black or homosexual; many blacks and homosexuals are customers of liberal newspapers, and no business wants to offend a customer.

But the same liberal newspaper or television news channel will pull some of its punches when it comes to reporting on the activities of government, even in Republican administrations, thus giving credence to the left critique, as in Michael Massing's "Now They Tell Us," about the reporting of the war in Iraq. A newspaper depends on access to officials for much of its information about what government is doing and planning, and is reluctant to bite too hard the hand that feeds it. Nevertheless, it is hyperbole for Eric Alterman to claim in "What Liberal Media?" that "liberals are fighting a near-hopeless battle in which they are enormously outmatched by most measures" by the conservative media, or for Bill Moyers to say that "the marketplace of political ideas" is dominated by a "quasi-official partisan press ideologically linked to an authoritarian administration." In a sample of 23 leading newspapers and newsmagazines, the liberal ones had twice the circulation of the conservative. The bias in some of the reporting in the liberal media, acknowledged by Okrent, is well documented by McGowan, as well as by Bernard Goldberg in "Bias" and L. Brent Bozell III in "Weapons of Mass Distortion."

The latest, and perhaps gravest, challenge to the journalistic establishment is the blog.

Journalists minimize offense, preserve an aura of objectivity and cater to the popular taste for conflict and contests by—in the name of "balance"—reporting both sides of an issue, even when there aren't two sides. So "intelligent design," formerly called by the oxymoron "creation science," though it is religious dogma thinly disguised, gets almost equal billing with the theory of evolution. If journalists admitted that the economic imperatives of their industry overrode their political beliefs, they would weaken the right's critique of liberal media bias.

The latest, and perhaps gravest, challenge to the journalistic establishment is the blog. Journalists accuse bloggers of having lowered standards. But their real concern is less high-minded—it is the threat that bloggers, who are mostly amateurs, pose to professional journalists and their principal employers, the conventional news media. A serious newspaper, like *The Times*, is a large, hierarchical commercial enterprise that interposes layers of review, revision and correction between the reporter and the published report and that to finance its large staff depends on advertising revenues and hence on the good will of advertisers and (because advertising revenues depend to a great extent on circulation) readers. These dependences constrain a newspaper in a variety of ways. But in addition, with its reputation heavily invested in accuracy, so that every serious error is a potential scandal, a newspaper not only has to delay publication of many stories to permit adequate checking but also has to institute rules for avoiding error—like requiring more than a single source for a story or limiting its reporters' reliance on anonymous sources—that cost it many scoops.

Blogs don't have these worries. Their only cost is the time of the blogger, and that cost may actually be negative if the blogger can use the publicity that he obtains from blogging to generate lecture fees and book royalties. Having no staff, the blogger is not expected to be accurate. Having no advertisers (though this is changing), he has no reason to pull his punches. And not needing a large circulation to cover costs, he can target a segment of the reading public much narrower than a newspaper or a television news channel could aim for. He may even be able to pry that segment away from the conventional media. Blogs pick off the mainstream media's customers one by one, as it were.

And bloggers thus can specialize in particular topics to an extent that few journalists employed by media companies can, since the more that journalists specialized, the more of them the company would have to hire in order to be able to cover all bases. A newspaper will not hire a journalist for his knowledge of old typewriters, but plenty of people in the blogosphere have that esoteric knowledge, and it was they who brought down Dan Rather. Similarly, not being commercially constrained, a blogger can stick with and dig into a story longer and deeper than the conventional media dare to, lest their readers become bored. It was the bloggers' dogged persistence in pursuing a story that the conventional media had tired of that forced Trent Lott to resign as Senate majority leader.

What really sticks in the craw of conventional journalists is that although individual blogs have no warrant of accuracy, the blogosphere as a whole has a better error-correction machinery than the conventional media do. The rapidity with which vast masses of information are pooled and sifted leaves the conventional media in the dust. Not only are there millions of blogs, and thousands of bloggers who specialize, but, what is more, readers post comments that augment the blogs, and the information in those comments, as in the blogs themselves, zips around blogland at the speed of electronic transmission.

This means that corrections in blogs are also disseminated virtually instantaneously, whereas when a member of the mainstream media catches a mistake, it may take weeks to communicate a retraction to the public. This is true not only of newspaper retractions—usually printed inconspicuously and in any event rarely read, because readers have forgotten the article being corrected—but also of network television news. It took CBS so long to acknowledge Dan Rather's mistake because there are so many people involved in the production and supervision of a program like "60 Minutes II" who have to be consulted.

The charge by mainstream journalists that blogging lacks checks and balances is obtuse. The blogosphere has more checks and balances than the conventional media; only they are different. The model is Friedrich Hayek's classic analysis of how the economic market pools enormous quantities of information efficiently despite its decentralized character, its lack of a master coordinator or regulator, and the very limited knowledge possessed by each of its participants.

In effect, the blogosphere is a collective enterprise—not 12 million separate enterprises, but one enterprise with 12 million reporters, feature writers and editorialists, yet with almost no costs. It's as if The Associated Press or Reuters had millions of reporters, many of them experts, all working with no salary for free newspapers that carried no advertising.

How can the conventional news media hope to compete? Especially when the competition is not entirely fair. The bloggers are parasitical on the conventional media. They copy the news and opinion generated by the conventional media, often at considerable expense, without picking up any of the tab. The degree of parasitism is striking in the case of those blogs that provide their readers with links to newspaper articles. The links enable the audience to read the articles without buying the newspaper. The legitimate gripe of the conventional media is not that bloggers undermine the overall accuracy of news reporting, but that they are free riders who may in the long run undermine the ability of the conventional media to finance the very reporting on which bloggers depend.

Some critics worry that "unfiltered" media like blogs exacerbate social tensions by handing a powerful electronic platform to extremists at no charge. Bad people find one another in cyberspace and so gain confidence in their crazy ideas. The conventional media filter out extreme views to avoid offending readers, viewers and advertisers; most bloggers have no such inhibition.

The argument for filtering is an argument for censorship. (That it is made by liberals is evidence that everyone secretly favors censorship of the opinions he fears.) But probably there is little harm and some good in unfiltered media. They enable unorthodox views to get a hearing. They get 12 million people to write rather than just stare passively at a screen. In an age of specialization and professionalism, they give amateurs a platform. They allow people to blow off steam who might otherwise adopt more dangerous forms of self-expression. They even enable the authorities to keep tabs on potential troublemakers; intelligence and law enforcement agencies devote substantial resources to monitoring blogs and Internet chat rooms.

And most people are sensible enough to distrust communications in an unfiltered medium. They know that anyone can create a blog at essentially zero cost, that most bloggers are uncredentialed amateurs, that bloggers don't employ fact checkers and don't have editors and that a blogger can hide behind a pseudonym. They know, in short, that until a blogger's assertions are validated (as when the mainstream media acknowledge an error discovered by a blogger), there is no reason to repose confidence in what he says.

The mainstream media, by contrast, assure their public that they make strenuous efforts to prevent errors from creeping into their articles and broadcasts. They ask the public to trust them, and that is why their serious errors are scandals.

A survey by the National Opinion Research Center finds that the public's confidence in the press declined from about 85 percent in 1973 to 59 percent in 2002, with most of the decline occurring since 1991. Over both the longer and the shorter period, there was little change in public confidence in other major institutions. So it seems there are special factors eroding trust in the news industry. One is that the blogs have exposed errors by the mainstream media that might otherwise have gone undiscovered or received less publicity. Another is that competition by the blogs, as well as by the other new media, has pushed the established media to get their stories out faster, which has placed pressure on them to cut corners. So while the blogosphere is a marvelous system for prompt error correction, it is not clear whether its net effect is to reduce the amount of error in the media as a whole.

But probably the biggest reason for declining trust in the media is polarization. As media companies are pushed closer to one end of the political spectrum or the other, the trust placed in them erodes. Their motives are assumed to be political. This may explain recent Pew Research Center poll data that show Republicans increasingly regarding the media as too critical of the government and Democrats increasingly regarding them as not critical enough.

Thus the increase in competition in the news market that has been brought about by lower costs of communication (in the broadest sense) has resulted in more variety, more polarization, more sensationalism, more healthy skepticism and, in sum, a better matching of supply to demand. But increased competition has not produced a public more oriented toward public issues, more motivated and competent to engage in genuine self-government, because these are not the goods that most people are seeking from the news media. They are seeking entertainment, confirmation, reinforcement, emotional satisfaction; and what consumers want, a competitive market supplies, no more, no less. Journalists express dismay that bottom-line pressures are reducing the quality of news coverage. What this actually means is that when competition is intense, providers of a service are forced to give the consumer what he or she wants, not what they, as proud professionals, think the consumer should want, or more bluntly, what they want.

Yet what of the sliver of the public that does have a serious interest in policy issues? Are these people less well served than in the old days? Another recent survey by the Pew Research Center finds that serious magazines have held their own and that serious broadcast outlets, including that bane of the right, National Public Radio, are attracting ever larger audiences. And for that sliver of a sliver that invites challenges to its biases by reading *The New York Times* and *The Wall Street Journal*, that watches CNN and Fox, that reads

Brent Bozell and Eric Alterman and everything in between, the increased polarization of the media provides a richer fare than ever before.

So when all the pluses and minuses of the impact of technological and economic change on the news media are toted up and compared, maybe there isn't much to fret about.

Books Discussed in This Essay

"Press Bias and Politics: How the Media Frame Controversial Issues," by Jim A. Kuypers. Praeger. Paper, $28.95.

"All the News That's Fit to Sell: How the Market Transforms Information Into News," by James T. Hamilton. Princeton University. $37.95.

"The Future of Media: Resistance and Reform in the 21st Century," edited by Robert W. McChesney, Russell Newman and Ben Scott. Seven Stories. Paper, $19.95.

"Coloring the News: How Political Correctness Has Corrupted American Journalism," by William McGowan. Encounter. Paper, $16.95.

"Now They Tell Us: The American Press and Iraq," by Michael Massing. New York Review. Paper, $9.95.

"What Liberal Media? The Truth About Bias and the News," by Eric Alterman. Basic Books. Paper, $15.

"Bias: A CBS Insider Exposes How the Media Distort the News," by Bernard Goldberg. Perennial/ HarperCollins. Paper, $13.95.

"Weapons of Mass Distortion: The Coming Meltdown of the Liberal Media," by L. Brent Bozell III. Three Rivers. Paper, $13.95.

Bloggers

The Light at the End of the Newspaper's Tunnel

By Phil Boas
The Masthead, April 1, 2005

It's customary for anyone writing to the uninitiated about blogs to define them. This is a journalism trade publication and you are no ordinary reader, so I'll spare you the customary definition.

Instead, I'll define blogs as they relate to you.

They are your Nemesis in the making.

If you've remained nonplussed as they took down Dan Rather and four of his Black Rock colleagues, if you haven't the slightest interest in acquainting yourself with the blogosphere, don't move an inch. You won't have to. Bloggers will be knocking on your door any day now. Or knocking it down.

To many of you, bloggers are a presumptuous rabble—amateurs elbowing their way into the publishing world. You may not know them, but they know you—your face, your manners, your prejudices, your conceits.

They're your readers. And, God help us, they've become the one thing we've always begged them to become . . .

Engaged.

The engaged reader in the world of cylinder presses and snail mail was much more manageable than the engaged reader in a wired world. Newspaper reporters and editors got their first glimpse of this not from bloggers, but from readers responding by e-mail.

Where once you could duke it out with a reader on the phone over the facts of a story or slant of a column, you now do so with pause when that reader is on e-mail.

You've learned from experience that the e-mailing readers can turn around and send every word of your dust up to the mayor, the governor, the competing newspaper, and your publisher.

That reader is now his own publisher.

If that was disconcerting before, it is ever more so with blogs.

Ask Nick Coleman, a columnist for the *Star Tribune* in Minneapolis, who has become a human shuttlecock batted across the Internet. He didn't like the withering critiques of his work by the amateurs at the Power Line blog (powerlineblog.com), so he fired back.

Rottweilers in Sheep's Clothing

"These guys pretend to be family watchdogs but they are Rottweilers in sheep's clothing," wrote Coleman. "They attack the Mainstream Media for not being fair while pursuing a right-wing agenda cooked up in conservative think tanks funded by millionaire power brokers."

The bloggers strongly denied the implication that think tanks or millionaire power brokers were behind the content on their website, and demanded Coleman produce his evidence.

The Power Line bloggers aren't journalists. They're attorneys whose pedigrees include Dartmouth, Stanford, and Harvard law. There is undeniable heft to their argument, so that to watch an exchange between the conservatives at Power Line and the lefty columnist at the *Star Tribune* is to watch an intellectual mismatch that is, frankly, embarrassing.

Likewise, Dan Rather thought he could stand down the bloggers. For twelve days he and CBS stonewalled on their now infamous scoop on George W. Bush's National Guard record. But with each day it became blindingly obvious that the story was constructed on myth.

The Power Line bloggers deserve and got much credit for becoming the information clearinghouse that ultimately exposed the fake memos behind the CBS story. But it was Charles Johnson on his blog Little Green Footballs (littlegreenfootballs.com) who I believe ultimately sank the CBS anchor. Johnson wasted no time in the days after the "60 Minutes" broadcast producing an exact duplicate of the CBS memos using the default font on Microsoft Word.

He then aligned copies of the so-called CBS original and his duplicate on his website, blinking them on and off alternately so the eye could see that everything—the font, the kerning, the leading, the superscript "th"—almost perfectly matched. CBS would have us believe three decades separated those two samples—one produced on a '70s-era typewriter and the other on a modern word processor. As was obvious to the eye, the charade was over.

To the CBS brain trust, Johnson's pulsing visual must have seemed the proverbial beating drum, drawing links from all corners of the Internet and demonstrating in utter simplicity that Dan Rather had been conned.

In those days when Rather was still stonewalling, you had to marvel at the confidence of the bloggers. They knew what Dan did not—that he and his network would ultimately blink.

Here's what newspaper editors and writers should know about this new Internet phenomenon. Bloggers don't have much respect for you. You are the "legacy media," the MSM. You're the Roman Catholic Church to their Martin Luther and his new high-speed cable modem.

To Hugh Hewitt (hughhewitt.com), the blogospheres leading cheerleader and one of its most polished practitioners, you are Stalingrad in 1944. Your institutions are hollowed out and your walls are scorched.

But of course, Stalingrad held, didn't it? And that gets me to the second definition of bloggers.

They are your light in the tunnel.

The Electronic Paradigm

The newspaper industry has known for a long time that eventually wood pulp would give way to microprocessors. That long-awaited paradigm shift now seems imminent. We may very soon be predominately an electronic medium, and that has many print executives on edge.

Newspapers have enjoyed some of the biggest profit margins of any industry for decades, and it is unclear if those can hold in a Web-based environment.

The newspaper industry has known for a long time that eventually wood pulp would give way to microprocessors.

Moreover, when you no longer need the millions of dollars in capital, the multimillion dollar press, the network of delivery people fanning out across the land, to start a newspaper, the door opens to competition.

If great gobs of capital will no longer separate you from that competition, what will?

Information. Or rather, the quality of your information.

We are headed to the Web in a big way, and our readers—especially our most engaged readers, the bloggers—are going with us. They are giving us a taste now of what our new environment will be like.

They will challenge and cajole us to confront our biases and our mistakes. And if we don't confront them, they'll clean our clocks.

They'll be our competitors and our colleagues and they'll force us to dig deeper into issues, think harder about them. They'll show us how to coalesce expertise on a breaking story and drill deeper for the more complete truth.

They're already teaching us today how to own up to our mistakes. You don't stonewall, as Dan Rather did. You fess up immediately and with full transparency. There's a lot of garbage on the blogosphere, but there is a high tier where the product is superior and is drawing mass readership. On those blogs, correcting error is part of the culture.

It has to be, explains mystery novelist and screenwriter Roger L. Simon on his blog rogerlsimon.com. "Bloggers—at least those with sizable audiences—are subject to more editing and fact-checking than virtually any mainstream media journalist. . . . I have written for *The New York Times*, *The Washington Post*, the *Los Angeles Times* and the *San Francisco Chronicle*—among others—and received nowhere near the amount of editing I get on here. I make a factual error on this blog, and I am often corrected within minutes."

If you listen closely, tuning in to the conversation beyond the oft-expressed contempt for mainstream media, you'll find the blogosphere actually needs mainstream media. We provide most of the coverage that starts the conversation. And by carrying the conversation further than we do, the blogosphere makes mass media vital.

The bloggers are demanding better standards and less bias—not unreasonable demands given journalism's current track record. But they're also creating stimulating and often irresistible discussion around the news we produce.

Journalism tomorrow, thanks to forces like the blogosphere, will grow more competitive. The best journalists will flourish. The mediocre will be exposed and washed out.

That's not something to lament. That's progress. We are living in the Information Age, when government and business are increasingly dependent on knowledge. It was inevitable that a knowledge-based culture would demand better, faster, more reliable information.

We're about to provide it, even if we get bruised in the process.

The Benefits of Blogs

By Michael J. Korzi
The Baltimore Sun, March 13, 2005

Recently, the first "blogger" was given credentials by the White House to attend the daily press briefings. The implication is that bloggers have a status similar to that of journalists. Naturally, this makes mainstream journalists react with hand-wringing, worrying that their professionalism is being compromised by "quasi-journalists," or worse.

Before addressing the larger issues of the relationship between bloggers and journalism, key concepts need to be made clear. "Blog" is short for "Web log" and generally connotes an online journal that is managed by one person or a group of individuals (bloggers).

Blogs considered collectively are the "blogosphere." As a blog is a journal, there are usually multiple daily postings to the Web site about contemporary events or issues, and links are provided to articles, news stories and other blogs.

The subject matter of blogs and the type of people who run them vary considerably. Many blogs are political, but others are devoted to sports, photography and medicine. Some bloggers have no expertise in their subject matter, while others have extensive knowledge and backgrounds.

Finally, blogs differ widely in their credibility. Some bloggers think little about the information they pass along or how they characterize it, while others worry greatly about what one might call ethical standards of presenting information.

As to the question of the relationship between blogging and journalism, journalists, or members of the "old media" (print news and major news networks), often make the case that blogging is a detriment to the public good. This argument often highlights two major disadvantages of bloggers: their bias and their lack of expertise.

Bloggers are characterized as being ideologically motivated (some of the most influential bloggers have been conservative) and therefore prejudiced in their presentation of information. Moreover, bloggers are seen as being neophytes, as people sitting at home in their pajamas—as one "old media" insider snidely put it in September—with little knowledge or experience reporting on critical issues.

Counterpoised to these bloggers are professional reporters with extensive backgrounds in subject areas and, what's more, journalistic training that promotes objectivity.

To be sure, some bloggers are biased and will pass along gossip or even blatantly untrue incidents; there are also many uninformed and inexperienced bloggers. But one can certainly find mainstream journalists who are partisan and who often opine on issues beyond their ken. The larger question is this: Are these "bad" bloggers outright liars or typical?

Most of the top political blogs and bloggers set rather high standards in their commentary and "reporting."

Most of the top political blogs and bloggers set rather high standards in their commentary and "reporting." And because of this, bloggers offer a critical service to journalists. While they will not and should not replace journalists—bloggers who think so are getting quite ahead of themselves—their influence is largely positive. Top blogs on the left and the right, such as Eschaton, Talking Points Memo, InstaPundit, *National Review*'s The Corner and Andrew Sullivan, to name a few, have set a high bar of credibility and illustrate that blogs and mainstream journalism together can contribute measurably to the public good.

Much of what these top blogs discuss and critique are stories produced by major journalists. While some bloggers are journalists, few see themselves as traditional journalists. Rather, they see themselves as commentators and public intellectuals. At any rate, they reinforce the work of other journalists even while they sometimes critique and question them.

Moreover, they discuss and provide links to such a large amount of information that they greatly aid readers in organizing and synthesizing information. Some Washington insiders are now seeing this virtue in blogs and start their mornings with a look at the blogs before picking up *The Washington Post* or *The New York Times.*

Further, blogs are more grass-roots than the mainstream media. Most top blogs are reader-friendly in that they communicate regularly with their readers (often posting comments and critiques from readers) or have "comments" sections on the blogs where readers can post the functional equivalent of a "letter to the editor."

This allows bloggers to quickly correct mistakes and get perspectives from individuals—some of whom are experts on the issues at hand—from all across America and the world. This is something at which the mainstream media are not particularly adept.

Finally and most important, bloggers (on both the left and right) watch the presentation of the news by mainstream journalists and offer critiques. They are like an additional layer of fact-checkers and bias-detectors. True, there is sometimes a witch hunt mentality among bloggers. But more often, they point out very real biases and mistakes in the presentation and characterization of the news, and in the process help to improve the work of journalists.

Mainstream journalists often see themselves as "surrogates of the people." Bloggers have shown the limitation of this characterization. Yet bloggers may also help to make the characterization more appropriate. Mainstream journalists should welcome the rise of blogging.

Are Bloggers Journalists?

BY TED LANDPHAIR
VOICE OF AMERICA NEWS, JULY 29, 2005

During the early days of the military conflict in Iraq, Americans discovered a new Internet phenomenon called "blogging." U.S. soldiers stationed in the Middle East created online Web pages, or "Web logs," to share their experiences and feelings with readers. This brought attention to blogging as a form of communication, and people worldwide began Web logs of their own. Last year, the "blogosphere," as the world of blogging is called, gained even more prominence when politically oriented bloggers exposed several mistakes in the media's reports during the U-S presidential campaign. VOA's Ted Landphair says bloggers' growing role as observers of the political scene has led to a provocative question: Are they journalists?

John Hiler, who edits a blog called "Microcontent News" that writes about blogs and the blogosphere, asked that very question a couple of years ago. Once bloggers go beyond venting their opinions and start researching and reporting information, do they qualify as "real" journalists? How can they? Mr. Hiler asked, when they don't have editors checking their facts, and when they openly harbor biases in favor of one political viewpoint or another.

Most blogs are highly personal—either talking about one's life experiences or sounding off about politics and world events. Bloggers often link to, and critique, each other as well. Internet users discover Web logs by chance, or at the recommendation of others. Or they can browse search engines such as "Feedster" and "Bloglines" that are specifically geared to blogs.

Bloggers are among the establishment media's most voracious readers and viewers, and prominent blogs regularly critique the mainstream media. In turn, the so-called "old media" are embracing new media like blogs. Many newspapers and television networks have assigned writers to produce blogs in the name of the paper or network.

Recently the debate about bloggers' qualifications as journalists has intensified. A discussion at the Heritage Foundation conservative think tank, for instance, was entitled, "Are bloggers and journalists friends or enemies?"

Jim Hill, who's the managing editor of the writers' group at the *Washington Post* newspaper, told the audience that bloggers are welcome in what he called "our band of journalistic brothers."

"A journalist can be anyone who takes pen to paper—how antiquated that phrase is in this electronic era—and spreads the news."

Danny Glover blogs about his personal life, such as the adoption of his children. But he also runs a mainstream online technology site for the *National Journal* magazine. In the Heritage Foundation discussion, Mr. Glover said many journalists have contempt for bloggers—calling them "barroom loudmouths," "salivating morons," and "the headless mob." He, himself, does not go that far. But he agrees that bloggers are absolutely NOT journalists.

"They are intellectual adversaries engaged in battle on a twenty-first-century information war. Are bloggers journalists? And the answer is a resounding 'no.' Bloggers are not journalists and clearly have no desire to be. They are grass-roots activists who, if inclined at all to quit their day jobs and change careers, are more likely to end up in political or policy circles than journalistic ones."

"Bloggers can move between journalist, pundit, critic, self-promoter, and back again, sometimes all within the same day."
—Ed Morrissey, a blogger

Danny Glover conceded that bloggers sometimes perform journalistic tasks such as checking the facts in politicians' statements. In that role at least, he said, they are important public watchdogs.

"But just doing journalism doesn't make you a journalist, any more than doing first aid makes you a doctor—any more than loaning money to a friend makes you a banker. Bloggers bring fresh insights, unyielding passion, and a whole lot of sass to the public sphere, and they answer to no one but themselves. They are the militiamen of the information revolution."

One of America's most successful bloggers is Ed Morrissey, whose conservative blog, called "Captain's Quarters," once crashed under the weight of twenty-thousand "hits," or online visits, a day. Bloggers dig for original information and exchange it with readers, he told the Heritage Foundation audience.

"And that's journalism, no matter what one calls a person delivering it."

"Captain Ed," as Mr. Morrissey is called in the blogosphere, acknowledged that bloggers often bring partisan biases to their work, and that moderate political bloggers are hard to find. But he argued that mainstream journalists also carry hidden—or not-so-hidden—political prejudices. When bloggers got together last year and debunked a CBS television report about President Bush's

Vietnam War service by exposing key documents as likely forgeries, Mr. Morrissey says, they were acting as "citizen journalists" in the best sense of both words.

"Bloggers can move between journalist, pundit, critic, self-promoter, and back again, sometimes all within the same day. As our own editors and publishers, we have the flexibility to do all that as we see fit. Our impact in all of these roles depends on our level of trust that we have built with our readers."

Journalism has long been recognized as a viable career and an honorable profession. A powerful one, too—so much so that it's often called the "Fourth Estate" alongside the executive, legislative, and judicial branches of government. Bloggers, on the other hand, rarely get paychecks. At best, they're sometimes called "amateur journalists." Most, like Ed Morrissey, blog at night, on weekends, or during breaks at work and must rely on unrelated fulltime jobs to pay the bills.

Blogger Jeff Jarvis once noted on his Web log called the "Buzz Machine" that journalism is "institutional, impersonal, and dispassionate." Blogs, he wrote, "are human, personal, and passionate." Too passionate and opinionated to suit many traditional journalists, who cling to the American tradition that only those who write objective news—and don't interpret it or intersperse their personal life stories, analysis, or partisan rants—can legitimately call themselves journalists.

Plugged-in Proust

Has E-lit Come of Age?

By Julia Keller
Chicago Tribune, November 27, 2005

Lovers of literature, be afraid. Be very afraid.

Let's modify that: Lovers of traditional literature—the stuff squashed between stiff or flimsy covers, arranged in clumps of typography and that remains as unassailable as stone tablets bearing sacred hieroglyphics—ought to be afraid.

Everybody else might be intrigued.

Literature, like all genres, is being reimagined and remade by the constantly unfolding extravagance of technological advances. The question of who's in charge—the producer or the consumer—is increasingly relevant to the literary world. The idea of the book as an inert entity is gradually giving way to the idea of the book as a fluid, formless repository for an ever-changing variety of words and ideas by a constantly modified cast of writers.

"There's a shift going on—people are going from being consumers to being co-creators," declares Scott Rettberg, assistant professor of New Media Studies at Richard Stockton College of New Jersey.

Adds William J. Mitchell, head of the Media Arts and Sciences program at the Massachusetts Institute of Technology, "All of these things are astonishing outbursts of popular creativity, unleashed by the electronic format."

Destinations

Blogs, e-mail, e-books, hypertext, text messaging, unbundling, Google Print—such terms, once esoteric, have shouldered their way into the common parlance.

Yet new technologies such as unbundling—a service recently offered by Amazon.com, in which customers can order portions of a book rather than the entire book—or Google Print, that company's plan to make the contents of more than 15 million books available online, would seem to apply to readers, not writers. The audience for literature, rather than literature itself, would seem to be affected.

Changing ways of accessing literature, however, could end up changing the way literature is produced. If customers increasingly nab their reading material by the phrase or by the page—rather than by the book—surely writers will eventually get the hint and begin to create works that capitalize on the new reality. Thus literature itself will undergo a dramatic retooling.

Or maybe not. Must the new always mean curtains for the old?

"I see all these things as coexisting," says Rettberg, a former Chicago resident who writes award-winning hypertext novels. "It's not like one technology comes along and replaces another. Things find their place in a new system.

"I teach New Media, but I also teach courses in print literature. I think of electronic literature as a continuation of many different genres of experimental literature in the 20th Century. I never thought hypertext would eliminate the book. The book will never go away."

Hypertext literature—computer-based works in which certain words, phrases or images are highlighted, encouraging readers to click on the links and indulge in digressions from the main text—is "finding a place in writing programs," Rettberg reports.

The rise of blogs is a positive sign, he adds. "I watch how the students here use their computers. It used to be mostly games. But now, there's a real self-conscious identity creation—it's blogging and social networks. People are creating their own music and art."

Mitchell agrees that blogs are an important new genre, one that puts consumers in control of content in fascinating and innovative ways.

"Blogs are pretty significant. It's a popular art form. It's folk art—it has the inconsistency, but also the vigor and energy, of good folk art. It's very powerful."

> *"E-mail should not be taken too lightly as literature."*
> —**William J. Mitchell, head of Media Arts and Sciences at MIT**

Both Ways

Mitchell's books are published simultaneously in print and online. And that's his vision for the future of literature: Not one delivery system crowding out another, but a variety of systems sharing space on the literal and virtual shelf.

He's also a big fan of e-mail and text messaging. "E-mail should not be taken too lightly as literature," Mitchell muses. "It's an incredibly vigorous literary form that's practiced by millions every day.

"Text messaging has a haikulike character. I think it's an expression of the vitality of language, of the urge people have to express themselves."

But what about the long narrative works—fiction and non-fiction—that traditionally are associated with the notion of literature? Will "Moby Dick" become a hypertext with links to Herman's Hermits and Starbucks? Will "Hamlet" be reduced to a text message ("2B/N2B")?

Mitchell and Rettberg say no.

"There's a place for electronic literature but the book won't go away," opines Rettberg.

Adds Mitchell, "Traditional paper-based literature survives where it makes sense . . . a book is a beautifully designed artifact. Fun to read. Convenient. It feels good, it looks good—it really works.

"All of these new formats just enrich and democratize literature."

Who Will Have the Last Word on Digital Frontier?

By Mandy Garner
The Times Higher Education Supplement, November 25, 2005

November has seen the trusty tugboat of academic publishing buffeted by a tidal surge of online book schemes. For some, announcements by Amazon, Microsoft, Random House and Google that they are to make sections of books accessible online are nothing short of the end of publishing as we know it. For others, such as many academic publishers, it is a chance to reach a wider audience.

Some academics, however, fear it will lead to more dumbing down because students will simply download chapters and paste relevant passages into their essays.

The announcements follow Google Print for Libraries' controversial decision to scan the content of university library books without seeking permission from publishers for material still in copyright, arguing that publishers have to opt out of, rather than in to, the scheme.

This month Amazon released details of its Amazon Pages programme, to be launched next year, which will allow readers to buy both chapters and entire books online. This builds on its existing "Search inside the book" facility. Unlike Google Print, Amazon says it will ensure that copyright is protected and will also allow publishers and copyright holders to set the charge.

A week later Microsoft said it was joining web search engine Yahoo! in a consortium, the Open Content Alliance (www.opencontentalliance.org), that plans to scan millions of public domain books from university libraries and other archives. The alliance includes some universities.

Microsoft also announced MSN Book Search, due to start next year, which will allow readers to find content from books, academic materials, journals and other print resources. And last week *The Wall Street Journal* reported that Google had approached a publisher about renting out online copies of books for a week at a charge of 10 per cent of the book's list price.

Publishers are rushing to respond to the plethora of schemes to ensure they do not miss the latest dot-com boat.

Oxford University Press is involved with Google and has its own subscriber-only cross-searchable database of, to date, 1,000 titles (www.oxfordscholarship.com).

Random House has gone a step further and is setting up a pay-per-page e-book scheme that authors can opt out of. Web providers will have to pay the company four cents a page for fiction and narrative non-fiction; access will be negotiated on an individual basis. Richard Sarnoff, president of corporate development, says the company felt it was better to take control of content provision rather than "reacting to business models proposed to our industry by e-tail, search engine or software companies."

Meanwhile, in October the Holtzbrinck Publishing Group, which owns Macmillan, launched plans for an online repository for digital book content in an effort to control web access. Jayne Marks, chief executive of global operations at MPS Technologies (a division of Macmillan), says search engines could look at files on the repository, but Macmillan would have control of copyright and security.

She adds that academic books lend themselves to digitising more than other books and that publishers have to be "realistic" about the fast-changing market.

"We are talking with a range of publishers and other digital providers, and are looking to bring as many parts of the industry together to come up with protocols and so on. You can't be an island on the web. We have to work together," she says.

The Association of Learned and Professional Society Publishers welcomes such collaboration and is hopeful that the Google Print situation can be resolved. The association and others recently met with Google and all agreed that European law—unlike US law, where publishers have taken out a legal case against Google—was clear that the search engine could not copy books without first obtaining copyright permission.

"We are working with them to enable them to get that permission in a practical way," says Sally Morris, the association's chief executive. She thinks proposals to allow online access to sections of books is "a natural extension of what has been happening in journal publishing," but adds that it would be interesting to find out how much people are willing to pay for such excerpts. "A one-price-fits-all policy won't fit. Chapters from expensive books cannot cost the same as those from other books."

Morris also believes that the ability to sell smaller parts of books online will lead to greater experimentation. "It lends itself to the way people work in universities. Teaching and learning is becoming more about putting together pieces of this and that rather than ploughing through a single course book." She adds that publishers such as Pearson already allow people to "custom-build their own books" by putting together a chapter here and a journal article there.

Not all academics agree with such views. June Purvis, professor of women's and gender history at Portsmouth University, says: "Selling a chapter or section of a book is symptomatic of our sound-bite culture; a little bit of this, a little bit of that."

David Cesarani, research professor in history at Royal Holloway, University of London, is "ambivalent" about online developments. "From an academic teaching perspective, in some ways it is no different from setting pages from a book for class reading or photocopying segments of a book for students. But there are crucial differences.

"In the scenario proposed by Amazon, there will be no course tutor to provide a context for the selected bits. Who will make the selections and on what criteria? The result could be dumbing down rather than broadening the readership."

Rob Singh, a politics lecturer at Birkbeck, University of London, adds that much depends on how universities approach internet development. "If courses are developed with an exclusive menu of online sources, the impact could be substantial," he says.

> *"Selling a chapter or section of a book is symptomatic of our sound-bite culture; a little bit of this, a little bit of that."*— June Purvis, a professor at Portsmouth University

Although many authors welcome the possibility of reaching more readers through web search engines and other providers, they are dubious as to whether this will generate more sales. Mark Le Fanu, general secretary of the Society of Authors, says: "Amazon claims it is like browsing in a bookshop, but you can't copy or cut and paste in bookshops. They claim you cannot download the page, but this has to be taken on trust. They also claim that it will promote sales and that they have the statistics to prove it, but we doubt their validity because they have been promoting the books for which they have a search facility."

Responses to the society's survey of major publishers about online developments have been polarised. There are textbook publishers who remain "very cautious" and academic publishers "who have embraced Google Print and feel it will give them greater exposure," says Le Fanu. He adds that authors need to be involved in any discussions about developments.

Anne Hogben, assistant general secretary of the Writers' Guild of Great Britain, says academic authors are "already heavily exploited by publishers" who benefit from academics' need to publish for career advancement. "They often get bad deals and sign away their rights, so they are not in a strong position."

She adds that, in the case of e-publishing, technically books will never be out of print so writers could sign away their rights for ever. She also believes that, as with the music industry, online access will lead to more emphasis being placed on live performances such as talks at literary festivals. "It's difficult now to be a writer who wants to be private," she says. "It's all about celebrity, getting your name around."

III. New Media and Entertainment

Editor's Introduction

Closely related to the publishing industry is the entertainment industry. Indeed, the two overlap. After all, books have always been—and news has become—a form of entertainment. Nevertheless, entertainment has been accorded its own section in this volume because the effects of the new media on entertainment companies are not quite the same as those on print publishing. There are two reasons for the difference. First, individuals who produce simple forms of entertainment, post their creations on the Web, and find an audience are not too great of a threat to mainstream media companies, whose success depends on offering expensive, high-quality products. Average people simply cannot afford to produce competitive television shows and movies. Second, the works they can produce—podcasts and songs, for example—do not challenge those being put out by media giants in quite the same way as blogs challenge the work of journalists: The homemade song or radio program is simply another item on the market and does not, as many blogs do, seek to question the value of its mainstream competitors. The new media, rather than offering people the chance to compete with major companies, is offering them other freedoms.

Chris Gaither's "Years After Giant Flop, Online Media Take Hold" discusses what media giants are doing to accommodate themselves to the changing broadcasting world. Most observers, Gaither points out, believe that new-media platforms will "support and expand" traditional media, not compete with it. The real advantage to the public of the change, he goes on to suggest, is that entertainment vehicles formatted for new-media platforms are affording consumers greater choices. A favorite television show, for example, need no longer be watched at a time predetermined by a network or on a particular device; shows can be stored and watched later on a variety of platforms, including home computers and iPods.

Consumers do not have to rely on media giants to provide entertainment, although the alternatives are unlikely to challenge mainstream vehicles as radically as they have in the news industry. One new-media platform, the podcast, a form of Internet radio, allows producers to circumvent the usual channels to get on the air. Robert P. Laurence examines this phenomenon in "Podcasts Provide a Sound Salvation for Early Radio." As he discusses the variety of podcasts being made by both private and corporate producers, Laurence suggests that broadcasting is becoming as fluid as print publishing. "With just a little extra computer know-how, anybody can produce a homemade radio show and send it around the world." Major broadcasters, he goes on to note, are attempting to dominate the field, but "the adventure, the real fun, is in finding the unpredictable unknowns, the amateurs with nothing but a microphone, a home computer and a dream."

In "Mixed Signals over Mobile TV," an article about the convergence of television programming and mobile phones, Alex Benady examines the excitement new-media platforms have brought to the entertainment industry, pointing out that the industry itself is largely responsible for the changes taking place within it. That, of course, is not the whole story. Companies are in the business of making money, and Benady does briefly take up this fact. The next article, "Downloading for Dollars: The Future of Hollywood Has Arrived" by Edward Jay Epstein, addresses the financial side of producing programming downloadable to computers, handheld devices, or TiVo-type digital recorders and how this will alter not just the way television and movies are consumed, but also the strategies companies employ to sell them.

Having focused on the changing social and corporate landscape engendered by new-media technologies, the chapter now takes a look at the effects of technology on art, examining one of the new forms it has made possible. John Leland's "The Gamer As Artiste" surveys the debate over the nature of video-game art. Are such creations a narrative art that should be developed into a genre capable of affecting players' emotions, or does their aesthetic power come from their metaphorical nature, rather than their ability to achieve realism? Whatever the result of this debate, which is already producing schools of video-game artists, video games have gained importance as cultural objects. They have become, according to James Paul Gee, a professor of education at the University of Wisconsin at Madison and author of *What Video Games Have to Teach Us About Learning and Literacy*, "the major cultural activity of the generation 30 or 35 and below, the way movies and literature were for earlier generations," Leland reports.

The final selection in this chapter, "And Now a Word from Our Sponsor. Our Only Sponsor" by Stuart Elliott, offers another analysis of how corporations are developing new ways to capture the public's attention. Corporations are not relying on radical new commercial models but are revisiting old ones, particularly the long-defunct custom of having a single advertiser sponsor an entire program. The movement has already produced a partnership between MTV and Mitsubishi, which is sponsoring MTV's MHD, a high-definition music channel, and between E! Entertainment Television and America Online, which is sponsoring E!'s *The Gastineau Girls*. The concept, Elliott points out, "is spreading to new media like podcasting, so-called online Webisodes and mobisodes, which play on mobile phones," proving that innovation is often produced not through rejecting the past but by appropriating it.

Years After Giant Flop, Online Media Take Hold

By CHRIS GAITHER
LOS ANGELES TIMES, JUNE 30, 2005

To watch most of his favorite programs, James Finn doesn't turn on the TV. He boots up his computer.

The 25-year-old manager of a Baltimore movie theater spends as many as four hours a day on ManiaTV.com, checking out music videos, extreme sports highlights and short films streamed over the Internet.

"I used to watch TV three or four hours a day," Finn said. "Now I'm down to about two hours of TV a week."

Five years ago, at the height of the dot-com boom, entrepreneurs and visionaries predicted that new online venues would overtake traditional media as viewers like Finn enjoyed shows and other content tailored to their tastes and schedules.

It didn't happen.

High-speed Internet connections were rare, and few people were willing to wait hours for a 10-minute video clip to download. Plus, most people's idea of on-demand entertainment was a drive to the local video store. The brutal tech bust seemed to close the book on the aspirations of those who envisioned the Internet transforming the way news and entertainment were produced and consumed.

But it turns out the dot-com crash may just have been the prologue. After licking their wounds, a rash of companies—including small players such as ManiaTV, Web giants such as Yahoo Inc. and traditional media titans such as Walt Disney Co.—are again investing heavily to bring more audio and video to the Internet.

This time, though, few people expect a crash because the companies are making money, capturing audiences and, yes, transforming the way news and entertainment are produced and consumed.

Technology has improved. People have grown accustomed to getting news on their BlackBerries and watching video on their computers. And old-media giants are working with the new-media leaders to make changes more soberly.

More than 20% of people who read newspapers rely primarily on online editions. Consumers watched 2.9 billion music videos, live performances and interviews on the Yahoo Music website last year. Apple Computer Inc.'s iTunes Music Store sells 40 million songs a month.

Google Inc., which sells online ads, vies with Time Warner Inc. as the world's most valuable media company. Advertisers spent $9.6 billion to place ads online in the U.S. last year. That's still only 6% of all ad spending, but it's growing fast.

Rather than supplanting traditional media, the Internet is viewed as a way to support and expand it.

"The competitive arena is only going to expand," said Patrick Mahoney, an analyst who follows consumer technologies for research firm Yankee Group. "I don't think consumers are completely shifting away from traditional entertainment, but they are starting to shift the time spent and money spent" onto the Internet.

Traditional outlets—newspapers, magazines, radio, television—still dominate most people's media diets and soak up most advertis-

---

Rather than supplanting traditional media, the Internet is viewed as a way to support and expand it.

---

ing dollars. And analysts caution that it will be a long time before new media rival the old. Among the challenges: increasing broadband penetration, making home networks easier to set up, getting devices from different manufacturers to work together better, ironing out thorny copyright issues and figuring out new business models.

But big media companies, which are likely to dominate online entertainment, are acquiring Internet upstarts at a furious pace. The most recent: Viacom Inc.'s MTV Networks last week snapped up youth website Neopets.com for $160 million. The following day, Time Warner's America Online began offering free ad-supported music and short films once available only to its subscribers.

Those who survived the dot-com bust largely agree that their vision of the Internet transforming media wasn't wrong, just a little early.

"People have realized it's not going to happen overnight," said Steve Wadsworth, president of Walt Disney Internet Group. "It's more of an evolution than a revolution."

What's changed? A lot.

- Half of U.S. homes with Internet accounts are connected at high speed. Last time around, Internet companies had to force content down dial-up connections, meaning it could take hours to download even a short movie. With fast connections, people have become more used to watching video online, and software advances have made the images much crisper.

- Living-room devices such as TiVo Inc.'s personal video recorder and Microsoft Corp.'s Xbox video game console are bridging the gap between the Internet and the television. With wireless networks, photos, songs and video files can be moved around one's home and watched on the most convenient screen.

- Mass entertainment is being fractured into thousands of customizable programs that can be watched or listened to anytime and anywhere. TiVo's recorder and Apple Computer's iPod blew up the traditional methods for delivering media and gave consumers a taste for getting personalized content on their own terms.

- Chip makers are building connectivity into the silicon that powers devices, making cellphones and hand-held computers capable of many tasks once reserved for PCs. Faster wireless data networks have spurred a flurry of deals between content providers and mobile companies, such as music service Napster Inc. and cellphone maker Ericsson, that let people turn to their phones' tiny screens for news and entertainment. Millions of digital cameras, cellphones and portable game consoles have ways to connect to one another and to the Internet.

- There's more interesting stuff to watch and listen to. The recording industry makes almost all of its new music available via paid downloads or online subscription services, and Internet giants are pushing movie and TV studios to follow suit. Yahoo and AOL are starting to create original Web-only programming of their own. Advertisers and consumers are creating their own short films that are spread by e-mail.

- And, perhaps most importantly, there's money to pay for all this online media. Advertisers are diverting more of their budgets to the Internet and other interactive media in search of consumers. Yahoo, Google, AOL and Microsoft's MSN—the four biggest online media players—each reaped more than $1 billion in advertising revenue last year, and all are growing fast.

ManiaTV Network Inc., for instance, is less than a year old but attracted 1 million viewers last month. That's enough to bring in some high-profile advertisers from broadcast TV, including Levi Strauss & Co., Dodge and the U.S. Navy.

"We looked at it and said, 'This is MTV 20 years ago,'" Levi spokeswoman Amy Gemellaro said.

Entrepreneur Drew Massey hatched the idea for ManiaTV in 1998, as many companies were spending furiously to get people to watch video clips on their computers. He knew they were onto something, but he didn't think the world was ready.

Massey waited to start the company until broadband connections reached 20 million households—the same threshold cable television reached before advertisers took it seriously.

"We're tapping into a 60-year-old business model, but we're using a new distribution method," Massey said. "This distribution method happens to be interactive, worldwide and incredibly addictive for the youth market."

It's not just young, tech-obsessed men who like to slice and dice their media.

Megan Walker, a 34-year-old high school English teacher who's on leave to care for her 7-month-old son, Ethan, discovered this spring that she could download individual songs through iTunes instead of buying whole albums. And her TiVo has been a revelation.

"I hate TV," she said. "But I do love one TV show: 'Six Feet Under.' I can watch it whenever I want, especially now that I have a baby. We only put it on after he's in bed. The downside is that I end up watching more TV than I would like."

Thanks to digital media, movies and shows are spreading to gadgets other than the living room TV set.

Thanks to digital media, movies and shows are spreading to gadgets other than the living room TV set. This month, TiVo teamed up with Microsoft and Intel Corp. to launch a feature that lets users transfer recorded shows to devices that run Microsoft's Windows Media Player software, including portable video players, fancy phones and hand-held organizers.

The transformation is a risky proposition for the major Hollywood studios. It threatens to give upstart entertainment companies a direct route into the home outside the control of broadcast and cable networks. It also has put a trove of bootlegged movies and TV shows within easy reach of people around the globe.

The Supreme Court ruled this week that file-sharing companies could be held liable for their users' piracy, but almost no one in Hollywood or Silicon Valley thinks illegal swapping of music and video is going away.

Rather, a number of studio executives believe that if they make movies and programs more accessible online, the public will buy more, and their marketing and production budgets will help them dominate the new pipelines just as they have dominated the old ones.

Until the content-protection and home-networking issues get worked out, small companies are the ones turning heads at Hollywood studios with their commitment to personalizing the delivery of video. Firms like ManiaTV and AtomShockwave Corp., whose AtomFilms.com shows short movies, "might be under the radar, but they are very clearly on the radar of the majors as to best practices," said Paul Campbell, a Microsoft business-development executive working with the entertainment industry.

Online animation studio Mondo Media, for instance, stopped work on almost all of its cartoons after the bottom fell out of the Internet advertising market in 2000 and 2001.

The exception was a cartoon series called "Happy Tree Friends," the dizzily bloody tales of forest animals that meet decidedly unhappy ends. Mondo kept churning out episodes, confident that the show could build a big audience online and that advertising would rebound.

"Happy Tree Friends" now draws 15 million unique viewers a month—enough to persuade advertisers to pay $300,000 or more for the commercial slot in front of each monthly episode. Mondo has sold half a million copies of "Happy Tree Friends" DVDs, not to mention a rich bounty of "Happy Tree Friends" merchandise.

That gets the attention of traditional media companies.

"The digital age is upon us," incoming Disney Chief Executive Robert Iger said at a recent conference for investors. "It's vital for us to migrate . . . to new media platforms."

In the meantime, Web giants are trying to drag more big-media programming online so they can draw more advertising. They're also making plans to create their own multimedia content.

The biggest Internet portal, Yahoo, has shifted many executives from its Sunnyvale, Calif., headquarters to a massive new office in Santa Monica, seeking to persuade Hollywood to promote and distribute more shows, films, music and games online. Yahoo CEO Terry Semel, former chairman of the Warner Bros. movie studio, hired several top entertainment-industry executives, including Lloyd Braun, former chairman of ABC Entertainment Television Group, to run Yahoo Media Group.

AOL, the world's biggest Internet service provider, is taking more dramatic steps, revamping its business in a bid to cash in on the online ad boom. In addition to moving much of its music and video programming outside the "walled garden" once reserved for AOL subscribers, it's also creating original programming—something industry watchers expect Yahoo to do as well.

"Convergence—that terminology fell out of favor," said Ted Leonsis, vice chairman of America Online. "But you're starting to hear people whisper it again."

Podcasts Provide a Sound Salvation for Early Radio

By Robert P. Laurence
The San Diego Union-Tribune, October 18, 2005

A new technology is reviving an old form of entertainment.

It's podcasting, it's booming in popularity, and it's returning real, old-fashioned radio shows to computer radio.

Radio has been moribund for more than half a century, relegated since the rise of television to music, talk, news, talk, sports, talk and talk. No more "Duffy's Tavern," no more "Fibber McGee and Molly," no more "John's Other Wife."

But with a home computer and a Google search of the word "podcasts" (coined from "iPod" and "broadcasts,"), anyone can find "Rockland County," a new radio soap opera, and listen to it at anytime. The latest episode of "Guiding Light," the CBS soap that started on radio in 1937 and has been playing daily on television since 1952, also is there for the listening.

With just a little extra computer know-how, anybody can produce a homemade radio show and send it around the world. And it seems like everybody is doing it.

Podcasting is growing "faster than the Web, faster than blogs, faster than e-mail, faster than just about anything else," said Chris Spurgeon, who covers new media for public radio's "Weekend America."

Most podcasters are just talking, ranting on politics, food, sports, movies, TV shows. Because there are no time limits, many of them go on and on. And on. And on. Because there are no limits at all, their language can be pretty raw.

But there are also real radio shows—cooking shows, fantasy adventures, comedies, soaps with stories, actors and sound effects.

Even the San Diego Zoo is getting in on the act, creating a podcast that will serve as an online audio guide. Once completed, it'll be like the audio guides popular in museums, but available for download to home computers and digital audio players—and easy listening at the zoo. The first installment, a guide to the Monkey Trail, has been posted at podcast.net, and the zoo's techies are working on more.

Only a year old, the free-for-all world of podcasting is being called the "Wild West" of the broadcast business. Where it's going, nobody really knows. Nor does anybody know if, or how, there's money to be

---

Podcasting

Definition: Unlike with a traditional radio program, you can download a podcast to your computer and listen to it whenever you want, starting or stopping the program as you please. You also can put a podcast on a digital audio player and listen to it on the go.

Etymology: 2004; iPod + broadcasting

---

made from it. But commercial broadcasters are launching podcasts to promote their on-air programs, and record companies are using them to advertise new releases.

Podcasts—available via Apple's iTunes software, Podcast.net, Odeo.com and myriad other sites—mark a major advance over Internet radio. You can listen to Internet radio as it streams to your computer, and you can hear "Fibber" and other old faves on old-time-radio Web sites. But a podcast has an added advantage: You can download it to your computer or digital music player whenever you want and listen to it at any time. The phenomenon has been called "radio TiVo."

The revolution is about to extend to TV. Last week, Apple announced a video version of its iPod that can play music videos and TV programs. In a deal with ABC, iTunes will offer episodes of such ABC shows as "Desperate Housewives" and "Lost," for $1.99 each.

Already, major broadcasters—CNN, NPR, Fox News, ESPN, ABC and others—are podcasting audio from dozens of news and entertainment shows from radio and TV, most without the commercials.

But the adventure, the real fun, is in finding the unpredictable unknowns, the amateurs with nothing but a microphone, a home computer and a dream.

Give a listen to "Cooking With Mary." You'll not only get to hear Mary explaining how to make breaded chicken cutlets, you'll hear her young son Jeffrey booming out his version of a deep, male radio announcer's voice: "OK, here it is! 'Cooking with Mary' podcast No. 1! And he-e-e-ere's Mary Nash!" Then, as Mary proceeds with her recipe, Jeffrey's baby brother cries lustily and persistently in the background while Mary presses gamely onward.

Mary doesn't say where she is. Many podcasts don't bother with such details. "The Anthony Show With the Lovely Alicia," for example, originates from "Anthony and Alicia's basement."

In one recent episode, Anthony related the life story of Bob Anello, an apparently fictional crooner: "This is the voice of the '30s, a voice that cried out in darkness and despair of the Depression, that showed new hope to a lost generation, a voice that made people laugh or cry. This is the voice of the beloved Robert Anello."

"Rockland County" is a New York City suburb and the title of a soap created by Roger Newcomb, 35, a Sun Microsystems business analyst.

> *Podcasting has been called "the Wild West of broadcasting."*—Ruth Meers, Podcast.net

He's been podcasting two five-minute episodes a week since March. "Rockland County" has 15 characters, and Newcomb's unpaid actors are mostly young professionals seeking to build their credits. But they're never together in a studio. He writes the scripts, then e-mails lines to each actor.

"Everyone records their lines separately," Newcomb said. "I have an 800 voice-mail line. I take their lines and splice them with other people in the scene, then I add music and sound effects, and it turns out amazingly well. The actors don't know what's going on with the other characters until they listen."

Brad Marcus podcasts "Sex, Drugs, Violence and General Hospital," his weekly summary of "General Hospital" plots that are laced with observations of a more personal nature: "So, anyways, last week's episode. Sorry about my substitute, the jackass. He's a bit of a loudmouth, and I will not be having him on the program ever again."

The podcasters' numbers have already grown beyond counting. "There are thousands of new ones every week," said Spurgeon of "Weekend America." "It's amazing when you consider that podcasting appeared on the radar maybe 12 months ago."

He added that there are also "real legal questions with playing music in a podcast. To do that involves either Draconian license fees you have to pay, or you . . . do it illegally. Which any big company won't do. But people who create popular podcasts do face this issue."

Podcasting has been called "the Wild West of broadcasting, but very professional-level people are also doing things," said Ruth Meers, in charge of customer relations at Podcast.net, based in Louisville, Ky. "It's giving people the ability and the creativity to do things they couldn't have done through traditional channels. Also, there's no FCC regulations."

Podcast.net, Meers said, created the first podcast directory last year. A spokesman for Apple, which began carrying podcasts via iTunes in June, declined to be interviewed.

Grant Baciocco, a stand-up comic from Burbank, and his pal Doug Price have already podcast 40 five-minute episodes of "The Radio Adventures of Dr. Floyd," a tongue-in-cheek time-travel adventure. They came up with the concept in 1999, as a cartoon series.

That idea didn't sell, Baciocco said, "but as soon as I heard about podcasting, I thought this is the perfect medium for this show, because it's automatically delivered to people."

He and Price write the show and perform most of the voices, along with a few friends whom he described as "low-level celebrities."

Ellen Wheeler, executive producer of "Guiding Light," said her show's heritage inspired her to launch a podcast. "We've evolved with television, but the show's roots are back in radio," she said. "So I just decided I would do it. There was no other dramatic television show putting their audio on podcast."

Podcasting proved to be a "perfect avenue" for the San Diego Zoo, which had been looking for a way to make audio tours available, said Web manager Inigo Figuracion.

One guide has been completed for the Monkey Trail, and another for Nairobi Village at the Wild Animal Park. "This is an ideal way of using tailor-made technology," Figuracion said. "Our goal is to have the entire zoo covered, and then visitors can download it to their own devices."

Mixed Signals over Mobile TV

By Alex Benady
The Guardian, November 28, 2005

It has been a fantastic few months—if you happen to be an insatiable TV junkie or trying to land a job in television. A flood of new technology, fancy-pants devices and "exciting industry initiatives" has washed over us meaning we need never again be more than a click away from Hollyoaks or Corrie. No matter where we are or what we are doing.

This month mobile phone operators Vodafone and Orange launched a mobile TV channel that broadcasts edited versions of all Channel 4 programmes via your phone. Vodafone also tied up a deal with Sky that will see Sky Mobile TV broadcasting 19 channels of content in downloadable five-minute chunks on to your handset.

Meanwhile, O2 has been testing something called DVB-H (digital video broadcasting-handheld), in partnership with NTL, that effectively turns your mobile into a fully-fledged digital television.

It won't be just viewers who benefit. This extraordinary technological explosion is about to trigger an employment boom that may even be comparable with the internet boom of the late 90s, say headhunters. "We are going through a period of mind-boggling growth. Companies that employed six people at the beginning of the year are now employing 50 or 60. They are looking for people across the board—creatives, account people, marketers and sales people," says Stephen Jardine of digital headhunting agency Cog.

While all levels of experience are needed, there is a particular shortage of middle-weight people with four or five years' experience, says Jardine. "Everything froze after the dotcom crash and people stopped hiring and training. As a result good people with a few years under their belt are commanding a real premium."

Record Spending Figures

It's a poorly-documented area, but an indication of the scale of upcoming digital demand comes from figures for internet advertising. UK advertisers spent a record £490m online between January and June this year, a 60% increase year on year and more than they spent for the whole of 2003, according to the latest figures from the Internet Advertising Bureau. On the consumer front, audience measurement body Barb says we watch an average of three and three quarter hours of television every day in this country.

Clearly big business is eager for us to watch a lot more in a lot more places. Yet evidence suggests most of us are not insatiable TV junkies. Corporate enthusiasm for ubiquitous TV 24/7 is not necessarily shared by viewers: a recent survey by media lawyers Olswang found that, of 1,500 people questioned, only 17% wanted to watch TV content on their mobiles, with 70% totally against the idea.

Another study by technology research firm Forrester found that only 5% of young people would definitely look for video content on their phones. People, it found, aren't so much interested in watching TV wherever they like, as whenever they like.

Despite consumer reservations, the proliferation of media platforms has led in particular to a surge in demand for media sales people. "The advertising potential of all these new platforms is so huge that the demand for salespeople is about to go through the roof," says Carl Dines, director of media recruitment agency Reilly People. But he warns that the new media demands a new set of skills in salespeople: "It's no longer just about selling space."

People . . . aren't so much interested in watching TV wherever they like, as whenever they like.

Sponsorship Opportunities

Commercial opportunities are much more integrated than they were. So people need to think in terms of selling space through sponsorship opportunities to driving through strategic tie-ups between companies. "A more entrepreneurial holistic approach is needed by candidates these days," says Dines.

So what are these companies playing at? Why are they trying to sell us something we don't seem to want and are unlikely to adopt? Some say mobile phone TV exists only because business, much like the rest of us, is intoxicated by the technology.

"Much that's happening now is being done simply because we have the technology to do it," says Paul Jackson, principle analyst at Forrester. He predicts that mobile phone TV will never really take off because you can't pay attention to a screen while on the move. And it will cost—the handsets are expensive and there are already too many competing incompatible technologies.

But this argument misses the point, say the broadcasters and phone companies. The former really don't care that much when or where people view their material—as long as they view. Robin Paxton, managing director of Discovery Channel, says: "There is a huge amount of technology-driven innovation at the moment. Some platforms will succeed, some will fail, but we are completely agnostic about which platform people choose to view on." The extra cost of providing material for mobile phone TV is relatively low, so why not try it, seems to be his argument.

The mobile phone companies make a similar point. Their TV initiatives are not designed to seize control of all TV viewing. These are just another extra feature to add value (and revenue) to current mobile telephone use. After all, no one accused oven manufacturers of moving into the clock market when they put timers on their products.

"Sky Mobile TV is a complementary service. It is not intended to replace mainstream TV," says a Vodafone spokesman.

However, the revenue from such services is rapidly becoming crucial to the survival of the mobile phone companies. "Income from infotainment is a fundamental part of our turnover," says Vodafone.

Whether it will be the nice little earner it is hoping for is still unclear. Vodafone says proudly that the 341,000 subscribers able to receive Sky Mobile TV dipped into it an average of three times each in its first two weeks alone. But currently the service is free. The real test will come in January when customers start paying £5 a month for it.

Downloading for Dollars

By Edward Jay Epstein
Slate, November 28, 2005

Once upon a time—two generations ago—the movie business was about making movies. Nowadays, it is about creating intellectual property that can be licensed in a raft of different markets. The Hollywood studios still make movies, of course, but by 2005, only 14.2 percent of their revenues came from movie ticket sales, while 85.8 percent came from licensing or selling their products for use in the home. (See Tables 1 and 2 for the studio revenue numbers.) Until 2005, the studio's principal access to the home market came through pay TV, free television, video rentals, and DVD sales. But now, with products such as Apple's video iPod and TiVo-type digital recorders becoming widely available, Hollywood is inching toward an even more lucrative way of exploiting the home market.

Disney's ABC network has already made a deal with Apple that will allow iPod users to download and watch shows, such as *Desperate Housewives*, for $1.99 an episode. The company has also been talking to Comcast about a similar pay-per-view arrangement for Comcast's 23 million cable subscribers. CBS, which is still controlled by Sumner Redstone, and NBC, a subsidiary of NBC Universal, have announced plans to release their programs for 99 cents a viewing whenever a customer wants to see them, through linkups with cable and satellite providers. Meanwhile, the satellite giant DirecTV, which Rupert Murdoch controls, is in the process of equipping its 12 million subscribers with TiVo-like digital video recorders that have extra storage capacity for eight hours or so of programming. Fox, which Murdoch also owns, can then download its shows onto an encoded section of subscribers' hard disks, which they can pay to view.

This downloading strategy is particularly appealing to the broadcast networks. Under long-standing FCC regulations, they have the right to negotiate with cable operators about carrying their programming. But, the broadcast networks rarely receive cash payment—instead they are compensated with such things as free ad time. Cable networks, such as ESPN, who are under no such mandate, get paid a hefty "carriage fee" for allowing cable operators to show their programs.* The networks, by offering their hit programs for downloading the next day, could also cash in on the cable audience. A cost of 99 cents a pop is hardly trivial when multiplied by an audience of 23 million Comcast subscribers. The networks are assuming—and this remains to be tested—that their regular audiences, which can watch the programs free, would have little incentive to wait a day and download them for a fee.

The studios stand to gain even more from a huge audience willing to pay to download movies from their libraries. Unlike DVDs, which require manufacturing, warehousing, distribution, and disposing of returns, it costs almost nothing to download a movie or cartoon. Indeed, all the costs of transmission would be born by the cable operator (or a site like the Apple Music Store), whose cut would be less, under present arrangements, than retailers get on DVDs. So, if a movie were a huge hit, such as *Shrek*, and millions of orders flooded in, the marginal cost of filling them would be zero. The consumer, once he bought the download, could watch it where and when he chose to just as he once watched a DVD.

The real issue for the Hollywood studios is how they can dig into this potential gold mine without undermining their existing revenue streams. Since the 1980s, the studios have managed their revenue by employing a system of "windows" to release their products to different markets. First, movies play in theaters, then, six months later, the video window opens, followed by the opening of the pay TV and then free television window. But giant retailers, to spur their seasonal sales, have been demanding their DVD delivery earlier and earlier, and they've thrown this system into turmoil.

With the possibility of costlessly providing millions of downloads to consumers of both their older and new films, the studio heads, including Disney's Robert Iger, are openly discussing radically revamping the window system. Obviously, if a home download of a movie were available at the same time (and price) as its DVD release, the download option might replace retail sales. To avoid that outcome, and a potentially dangerous confrontation with Wal-Mart, the studios would have to delay the download release until well after the DVD release. But while the studios may find this embarrassment of choices somewhat paralyzing at present, as more and more consumers get digital recorders or video iPods, downloading for dollars may prove irresistible—even if it means doing away with the windowing system.

Hollywood's downloading option, by whatever device it may be realized, is just one more part of the transformation of movies from a big- to a small-screen experience and from a theatrical to a home—or even mobile—product.

---

* Correction, November 29, 2005: This article originally and incorrectly stated that the FCC required broadcast networks to provide their regular programming free to cable operators. In fact, the FCC gives broadcast networks the right to negotiate with cable operators, but the result of such negotiation is rarely cash payment. The Hollywood Economist thanks reader Andrew Schwartzman for pointing this out.

Hollywood-by-the-(Secret)- MPA Numbers

Table 1, Studio Revenues Worldwide, 1948–2003 (Billions)

The Rise of the Home Entertainment Economy
Worldwide Studio Receipts
Inflation-corrected, 2004 US Dollars
(Billions of dollars)
Inflation-Adjusted in 2003 Dollars

Year	Theater	Video/DVD	Pay-TV*	TV, Free**	Total	Theater Share (%)
1948	7.8	0	0	0	7.8	100
1980	4.5	.2	.39	3.35	8.53	55
1985	3.04	2.40	1.07	5.74	12.2	25
1990	5.28	6.02	1.66	7.60	20.31	22
1995	5.72	10.9	2.40	8.13	27.22	20
2000	6.02	11.97	3.2	11.03	32.23	19.5
2003	7.68	19.4	5.71	11.7	42.27	17.9
2004	7.4	20.9	4	12.6	44.7	16.8
2005, 1st Q	1.71	5.95	1.09	3.3	12.05	14.2

* Includes both Pay-Per-View and Subscription Pay-TV
**Includes network TV, cable TV and local stations

The Rise of DVDs

Table 2

Global Home Video Sales
DVD & VHS
Studio receipts
(Billions of dollars)

Year	DVD	VHS	Total
1993	$0	$5.9	$5.9
1997	$0	$9.8	$9.8
2002	$10.39	$5.929	$16.3
2003	$14.9	$3.9906	$18.9
2004	$18.8	$2.1	$20.9
2005, 1st Q	$5.674.4	$.274	$5.95

The Gamer As Artiste

By JOHN LELAND
THE NEW YORK TIMES, DECEMBER 4, 2005

Last week, I spent several days living—and dying—inside the new Xbox 360 console, with four popular games pegged as particularly cinematic. I entered as a curious novice, less concerned with breaking the games than with exploring the worlds they opened, and the worlds you die in.

I died as a princess in a green miniskirt, as a space warrior, a World War II soldier named Vasili and a humorless F.B.I. agent tracking a sadistic killer. My deaths, rendered in state-of-the-art detail, were not illustrious or mourned. They consisted of the limited repertoire of gestures assigned to death by the game makers. In the virtual world of games, players get to invent their own unique lives, but when they die, even the greats cede control to their maker.

The release of the Xbox 360 game console last month, with its sharper graphics, is likely to renew debates about whether games are too violent or too mindless, or whether children should be outside running around.

But as video play occupies more and more of American imaginative life, the games themselves raise other provocative questions: Can games be something more than games? In other words, can they move people emotionally or intellectually in the manner of great art?

Steven Spielberg last year offered one model for the medium to follow: cinema. In an address to students learning to be game developers at the University of Southern California, Mr. Spielberg, who has since contracted to create three games, challenged the industry to improve the storytelling, character development and emotional content in the same way it has enhanced the images and action. The medium will come of age, he said, "when somebody confesses that they cried at Level 17."

But movies are just one model for games to emulate. Henry Jenkins, director of the comparative media studies program at the Massachusetts Institute of Technology, suggested that they are equally close to dance, as a medium of performance, or architecture, as a medium of creating unique spaces.

Museum exhibitions, academic conferences and university curriculums have examined games as art. A 2004 conference at Stanford University called "Story Engines" looked at game play as a way of creating narratives, at a time when the audiences for established story vehicles like books, newspapers, movies and network television are in decline.

As games gain attention as an art form, it remains to be determined just what sort of art they can or should be. Are they like movies, projecting the vision of an auteur like Mr. Spielberg or Peter Jackson, who recently collaborated in "Peter Jackson's King Kong: The Official Game of the Movie"? Or are they more like the song "Frankie and Johnny," which is performed in different ways by many people, and in which the art lies in the sum of performances?

In a $10 billion industry, the stakes are high. Like the television set before it, the game console is now colonizing American living rooms and the lives therein. Americans spend more money on video games and consoles than on movies; nearly half the country plays. Thirty-three years after Pong, video games have become "the major cultural activity of the generation 30 or 35 and below, the way movies and literature were for earlier generations," said James Paul Gee, a professor of education at the University of Wisconsin at Madison and author of "What Video Games Have to Teach Us About Learning and Literacy."

Like the television set before it, the game console is now colonizing American living rooms and the lives therein.

Even among children who don't grasp the lessons taught in their schools, Professor Gee said, they "can all discuss the stories in video games at a very sophisticated level."

Like previous new game consoles, the Xbox 360 allows games to look more like movies. Walls have textures; battle scenes show remarkably detailed characters moving independently. Such advanced technology, made possible by increased processing power, also raises the cost of developing games, which now run budgets of up to $25 million, including the expenses of licensing characters and music. This in turn influences the type of games that are produced: Of the 10 top-selling games of last year, all were sequels to successful games, tie-ins to hit movies or both.

This emphasis on realism, in what is inherently an artificial medium, misreads what is special about the game experience, said Douglas Rushkoff, author of "Playing the Future: What We Can Learn From Digital Kids." Video games, he said, should be less like movies, not more.

"This is an age-old thing going back to Pong," said Mr. Rushkoff, who describes himself as an enthusiastic gamer. "What made Pong so exciting was not its accurate depiction of Ping-Pong or its relationship to reality. It was the ability to move pixels around on the screen, and an appreciation for the way the game designer is working in metaphor."

The relationship between the movie and game industries has always been bumpy. Though there have been lucrative crossovers between the two media, movies based on hit games are often duds, like the recent "Doom," as are games based on hit movies.

> *Some developers are taking advantage of the unique properties of games to tell stories.*

"The press treats Spielberg's announcement as the second coming," said Professor Jenkins of M.I.T. "But game designers remember how the game based on 'E.T.' nearly killed Atari, and is considered the biggest failure in game history."

In its emphasis on filling games with scenes and dialogue to establish character, Professor Jenkins said, "Hollywood puts its effort into things gamers don't care about."

He compared the video game industry to Hollywood of the 1930's, when studios created standards for their products but also imposed formulas for the movies they churned out, with rising budgets and diminishing creative risk-taking.

"What you need now is a garage band aesthetic, or independent film aesthetic for games," he said. "You're building the world from scratch. Why does it have to look like the world we live in?"

In fact, an indie aesthetic is starting to develop, cultivated by academia, online journals and a movement toward low-budget, "casual" games that stress simple images but complex game play. Eric Zimmerman of gameLab, which created a casual game called Diner Dash, said that the big companies were afflicted with "cinema envy." The impulse to make people cry, he said, was a "misguided idea of what emotional depiction is." He said, "Games are by nature incredibly emotionally engaging. Look at poker. There's emotional engagement, strategy and a Zen-level involvement. Games are dynamic, participatory systems. That's a level of storytelling that a film can't do."

So what can video games do that movies can't? For starters, it is a mistake to overlook the raw experience of play. But beyond the blockbusters that dominate the industry, some developers are taking advantage of the unique properties of games to tell stories. Professor Gee of Wisconsin cited a game being developed to help children sort through traumatic divorces, or an online game called Second Life that allows users to invent their own simulated environments, which other players can visit.

"If all we're doing is making the 17th version of a movie you've already seen, our culture isn't going to look very good," he said. "We haven't begun to scratch the surface of what games we could make without somebody shooting someone."

Though games may not produce Mr. Spielberg's tears, they are the one medium that allows users to experience guilt, because they make the player responsible for the actions of a character on screen, Professor Jenkins said. "If you do something despicable, you have yourself to answer for."

Few games exploit this potential, but there is nothing preventing future developers from doing so, he said.

But my own experience inside the box raises a different narrative possibility. In a culture that is squeamish about death, games are the first major medium that makes one's own mortality a central element in the experience. In many games, to reach the last level alive is to put the game behind you.

A challenge for game makers, then, is not to make users cry at the death of another, but to find meaning in their own. This is, after all, the one universal human condition. To which games add the one antidote: the ability to press restart.

And Now a Word from Our Sponsor.
Our Only Sponsor.

By Stuart Elliott
THE NEW YORK TIMES, December 5, 2005

For decades, first on radio and then on television, the phrases "And now a word from our sponsor" and "Brought to you by" were as commonplace as canned laughter. Shows even saluted their advertiser patrons by name, from "The Bell Telephone Hour" to "Magnavox Theater" to "Westinghouse Desilu Playhouse."

But by the late 1950's, rising costs along with concerns about control over programming produced profound change. Advertisers shifted from sole sponsorships to buying commercials one spot at a time all over the network schedules. (About the only exception: Hallmark Cards, which has continued to sponsor the "Hallmark Hall of Fame" since 1951.)

Now, as Madison Avenue anxiously seeks ways to catch the attention of jaded, distracted consumers, the idea of sponsorship and similar forms of advertising exclusivity is gaining favor again. And in a contemporary twist, the concept is spreading to new media like podcasting, so-called online Webisodes and mobisodes, which play on mobile phones.

"It really is back to the future," said Max Wasinger, senior vice president for sales and marketing at Mitsubishi Digital Electronics America in Irvine, Calif. His company, a unit of Mitsubishi Electric, agreed last week to become the exclusive sponsor of a high-definition music channel being introduced by the MTV Networks Music Group division of Viacom.

"This takes our brand and moves it to another level," Mr. Wasinger said of the deal, which includes Mitsubishi becoming the title sponsor of original programming on the MHD music channel and the words "Powered by Mitsubishi" appearing in spots urging viewers to watch.

The sponsorship offers Mitsubishi a way to "make a closer connection" than conventional commercials can, Mr. Wasinger said, with "a younger generation that is buying high-definition and big-screen television sets."

Among the other big advertisers signing on for sponsorships are Bacardi, ConAgra, DaimlerChrysler, Ford Motor, General Motors, Georgia-Pacific, Nike, Nokia, Royal Philips Electronics, Target and Time Warner.

"We realize the ability of a 30-second stand-alone spot to impact viewers has diminished," said Richard Taylor, senior vice president for brand marketing at AOL in Dulles, Va., part of Time Warner.

Sponsorships offer a marketer a chance to convince consumers that "a brand adds value to the viewing experience," he said, by providing benefits that could not be offered if the brand was, say, 1 of the 16 shown in the eight minutes of commercials in a 30-minute program.

For instance, AOL's sponsorship of the second season of the reality series "The Gastineau Girls" on E! Entertainment Television, which began last week, includes free podcasts produced by AOL with the stars of the series, Lisa and Brittny Gastineau. The 10 podcasts, one for each week of the series, can be downloaded from a Web site (aol.com/podcasting) where computer users may also subscribe to get all 10.

> *Sponsorships offer a marketer a chance to convince consumers that "a brand adds value to the viewing experience."*
> —Richard Taylor, an AOL executive

Also, when Philips agreed to be the sole national sponsor of "60 Minutes" on Oct. 23, the company ran about half as many commercials as are scheduled in a typical episode, allowing CBS to add about six minutes to the content of the show.

"We're always looking for opportunities where we can stand out in the clutter, and this was doing something the viewer would look favorably upon," said Andy Donchin, executive vice president and director for national broadcast at Carat USA in New York, the media agency owned by the Aegis Group that negotiated the deal for Philips.

"I looked on the CBS Web site after the show aired and people were writing in to say thank you," Mr. Donchin said, contrasting that with the usual attitude among consumers that commercials are "uninvited and intrusive."

Data from IAG Research gathered by CBS, owned by Viacom, showed that among viewers aware of the sponsorship, their favorable opinion of Philip increased by 38 percent.

To be sure, sponsorships are no panacea for the problems of how to reach consumers. And they must be developed carefully lest they produce new problems.

"You need to have sensitivity and be responsible," said Greg D'Alba, chief operating officer for advertising sales and marketing in New York for the CNN cable network owned by Time Warner.

CNN works hard to make sure viewers understand that an advertiser's sponsorship "is never going to change how we cover a story," he added.

Mr. Taylor at AOL said: "The last thing I'd want to do is dominate a program to the point it's annoying. You start to be an annoyance, and you're not doing anything to benefit the consumer—or the brand."

With sponsorships resembling more and more the model that originated decades ago, could the concept come full circle? That is, will advertisers soon agree to sponsor entire seasons of series and in exchange get their names in the titles?

"Yes, there are advertisers definitely interested and we are talking about that," said David Levy, president of the Turner Entertainment Sales Group in New York, which oversees ad sales for cable channels like Cartoon Network, TBS and TNT.

There is one caveat to the discussions, Mr. Levy said: unlike the early days of TV, when series were brought to the networks by advertising agencies and did not get on the air unless they had sponsors, "the networks now would not give up control of the creative and the schedules."

If advertisers are amenable to those stipulations, it may not be long before the TV listings include entries for shows like "The Cingular Cellphone Hour," "Microsoft Theater" and "Wachovia Playhouse."

IV. New Media As an Educational Tool

Editor's Introduction

Up to this point, this volume has largely treated the media as the communications industry, focusing on publishers and broadcasting companies. Some acknowledgment of other forms of media, such as video games, which many view as a narrative genre, has been made, but as in many discussions of the new media, the term has been employed in a limited sense. More broadly speaking, *media* includes any means of transmitting information, whether through pictorial art, literary fictions, factual reports, or other channels of communication. The rest of this book takes a broader view of the media, considering the impact of the computer revolution on areas of life in which the new media is not usually discussed. The current section looks at changes in the way educational material is transmitted, focusing on how technology is being employed to reinvigorate the student experience and, in some cases, turn classrooms into media outlets that reach beyond the school building.

"Remaking Liberal Education" by T. Mills Kelly discusses the challenge of effectively integrating technologies into the classroom and, more important, the potential for significantly increasing what students learn from their courses. Kelly argues that exposing students to the multimedia-educational environment of a network leads to the transfer of "control over the exploratory aspect of learning from the instructor to the student, freeing the student to pursue his or her own discoveries. When a student clicks on a hyperlink to a Web resource, she embarks on her own intellectual journey, the results of which neither she nor her instructor can predict in advance." And while questions remain about the effectiveness of affording students such an opportunity, so far the evidence suggests that the new media is positively affecting the learning experiences of students, despite such drawbacks as the "potential to scatter student thinking about questions posed by the sources they encounter."

Kimberly Marselas's "College Lectures Go Digital" and Patrick Beeson's "Bringing Blogs into the Classroom" consider the use of particular new-media genres—podcasts and blogs—and provide further anecdotal evidence of the advantages to students of turning classrooms into new-media environments. Recording lectures onto podcast, Marselas observes, gives professors an alternative to lecturing during class time and students a tool to reinforce lessons or hear lectures they have missed, thereby providing students with more options to engage with course material. Beeson's analysis of journalism courses found that the use of blogs in class improved the quality of the students' work, as the knowledge that their output would appear in a public forum created an incentive for them to do a good job. The public nature of assignments also led students to embrace a collaborative culture.

Turning from the classroom to the library, "Digital Archives Are a Gift of Wisdom to Be Used Wisely" by Roy Rosenzweig considers the advantages and disadvantages of Web-based research, arguing that for students in universities with small libraries, the Web provides access to collections comparable to those found in such eminent institutions as Harvard University. The Internet, therefore, can democratize education as never before. While he acknowledges that the Web is not a perfect resource, Rosenzweig nonetheless maintains that its advantages far outweigh its shortcomings. The errors or forged documents that find their way onto the Internet, for example, are eventually corrected or exposed by the Web community, and Web sites have been set up to direct students toward reliable resources, leaving only the difficulty of teaching students how to properly read the documents they find. However, the nature of the Web has been changing as research-based Web sites turn more commercial, which raises the possibility that the distinction between the collections available at large universities and those at smaller ones will reemerge in the digital world. Rosenzweig's concern then "is not that students will find junk online, but rather that they will fail to gain full access to the Web's riches or won't know what do with those riches when they find them."

The chapter concludes with Shelley Emling's "Classic Lit Goes Txt Msging," which considers a British cell-phone service's recent introduction of text-message versions or plot summaries of literary texts—*Romeo and Juliet*, for example. "The educational opportunities it offers are immense," John Sutherland, the literature professor who developed the program, has said. "You could shrink the whole five-act text of 'Hamlet' into a few thousand characters. And those few thousand characters could serve as a memory aide, enabling you to back-translate into the golden syllables of the original." Others are not so sure. Helen Hackett of University College London, for instance, denies that one can develop an understanding of a book without reading it. "[S]tudents who do well are the ones who love the language of literature, and love to write well themselves." Nevertheless, there are plans to publish, among other commonly studied literary texts, the complete works of Shakespeare and Geoffrey Chaucer's *The Canterbury Tales* in text-message format.

Remaking Liberal Education

By T. Mills Kelly
Academe, January/February 2003

In a speech to the American Historical Association in 1905, Harvard historian Charles Homer Haskins concluded that the "most difficult question which now confronts the college teacher in history seems, by general agreement, to be the first year of the college course." Haskins surely had no idea that his remarks would remain relevant at the beginning of the twenty-first century. And, although he spoke only about the history survey, Haskins might just as easily have been referring to any introductory course in the general education curricula.

Across the country, enrollments in introductory survey courses—the primary vehicle for giving students a dose of liberal learning—are growing rapidly. Although those of us committed to liberal education wish that this growth were a response to increased student demand, the reality is that ever-expanding general education requirements force many, if not most, of our students into a brief and sometimes painful flirtation with liberal learning. As a result, faculty teaching the introductory survey—in whatever discipline one cares to name—often find themselves face to face with students who wonder why they are in such a course and how they can escape with the least damage to their grade point average. Students understandably worry about how they can consume and internalize the mass of content thrown at them by an instructor trying to cover as much as possible in that one chance she has to expose students to her discipline.

As a humanist, I strongly support the goals of general education. So many of our students today bring intense pragmatism to their choice of courses and majors. If they were not forced to take a history course, a literature course, or a course in the arts, how many of them actually would do so? I suspect that the number is greater than our fears, but still far less than our hopes.

By exposing first- and second-year students to liberal learning, we hope that we will perhaps lure a few of them away from business, computer science, or engineering, and into the liberal disciplines. Along the way, we work hard to teach them something we like to call "critical thinking"; we acquaint them with the epistemologies of several disciplines, inculcate an awareness of and appreciation for diversity of all kinds, and educate them about how to communicate effectively—in speech, writing, images, and, lately, new media. A strong argument can be made that such skills and a broad intellectual horizon substantially improve a citizen's ability to function in our society. But many students do not get or are not given this message. Instead, many see the liberal arts, as represented by general education requirements, as an obstacle to be surmounted on the way to one's "real" studies.

New Media

Faculty and administrators across the country—on campuses large and small—understand the challenges of liberal education, which in many ways are much the same as those Haskins noted a hundred years ago. One challenge that he could not have anticipated, however, is the transformation of our campuses and curricula by new information technologies. Faculty increasingly feel pressure—from administrators, colleagues, and students, or within themselves—to infuse technology into their courses, as though a course Web site or a PowerPoint lecture will somehow improve learning just by its existence.

Many obstacles must be overcome before we can realize the potential of information technology to transform education.

Anyone who has tried to "ramp up" liberal learning on campus knows that many obstacles must be overcome before we can realize the potential of information technology to transform education. The learning curve required to use new media (beyond simply putting a syllabus up on the Web or creating a basic PowerPoint presentation) is steep, and only a minority of faculty come to this task with any prior training. Most of us simply do not have time to set aside from our teaching, research, or service to become adept users of these technologies.

The continued lack of sufficient technology infrastructure on most campuses means that only a few classrooms have the equipment necessary to permit students and faculty to maximize their experience with new media, and the competition for these rooms is often intense. Moreover, the share of new students on our campuses who come from economically and educationally disadvantaged backgrounds continues to grow, and many of these students lack the skills needed to take advantage of technologically enhanced learning opportunities.

As daunting as these challenges can be, and as familiar as they are, they are administrative problems that can be overcome by increased investment in curricular change, technology infrastructure, and the equalization of student access to technology. The path to their solution may be expensive, but it is not especially complicated.

Tradeoffs

More difficult to address is the potential of new media to transform liberal learning in substantial ways. New technologies offer students immediate multimedia experiences—simultaneous encounters with still and moving images, music, data, and text, for example—that conventional teaching cannot provide. This prospect alone presents a genuinely revolutionary possibility for teaching the liberal arts, especially if students pursue different lines of inquiry simultaneously and interactively in a networked environment.

Moreover, students' use of networked information transfers control over the exploratory aspect of learning from the instructor to the student, freeing the student to pursue his or her own discoveries. When a student clicks on a hyperlink to a Web resource, she embarks on her own intellectual journey, the results of which neither she nor her instructor can predict in advance. These "novices in the archive," to borrow a term from American studies scholar Randy Bass, can access, sort through, and analyze masses of data in ways that we could not imagine even ten years ago.

One of the best-known sources for teaching history and culture is the American Memory Project of the Library of Congress, which offers more than seven million digitized primary sources drawn from a hundred different archival collections. Powerful searching software permits visitors to this site to locate information within the collection through keyword and other searches. Such tools allow students to pursue their own lines of inquiry and to engage in the kind of research previously reserved for advanced graduate students and faculty.

At the same time, the interactive and hypertextual nature of new media has the potential to scatter student thinking about questions posed by the sources they encounter. Rather than considering each source carefully and critically, students may become so entranced by the prospect of flitting from one hyperlink to another that they do not engage all (or even most) of the possible meanings and implications of what they read, watch, or hear.

In addition, the tactile aspects of learning disappear when students sit at a screen. They can manipulate data, listen to music, watch a movie, or read text on the computer (although most of them still print out the texts assigned online). But they cannot touch. The very medium that brings unprecedented quantities of information and analysis to students' desktops interposes a barrier between them and the artifacts with which we ask them to grapple.

There are other tradeoffs when it comes to infusing new media into a course. At the heart of these tradeoffs is an important question we have yet to answer: when new media are added to a course, do our students learn better, more, or differently? In other words, is there some sort of measurable beneficial outcome from all the time and money invested in introducing technology into a course? After all, if we cannot point to improved or different learning, then we will have wasted both our time and that of our students.

Fortunately, researchers across disciplines—history, English, chemistry, and mathematics, among others—are inching toward answers to this vexing question. And their answers are rooted in their own epistemologies, rather than being the sole property of cognitive psychologists and schools of education. Although some of this research is being conducted by individuals working in isolation, much of the inquiry is occurring in collaborative endeavors like the Carnegie Academy for the Scholarship of Teaching and Learning <www.carnegiefoundation.org/CASTL/index.htm> and the Visible Knowledge Project based at Georgetown University <crossroads.georgetown.edu/vkp.>

Greater Transparency

As a participant in both of these efforts over the past several years, I can say that the researchers affiliated with the projects have framed some of the right questions to ask about technology

---

The very technologies we are experimenting with are expanding our understanding of their utility for teaching our students the liberal arts.

---

and liberal learning; some have even begun to offer interesting, albeit tentative, conclusions. I have been able to show that Web-based assignments can induce greater recursive reading of sources, in which students return repeatedly to the sources assigned, often rethinking their first analysis in light of later learning. Similarly, Sherry Linkon's students at Youngstown State University have demonstrated a deeper understanding of the interdisciplinary concepts central to American studies as a result of certain exercises in new media that she created for them. These small successes did not, however, merely result from the adoption of technology in a course. Rather, they grew out of carefully designed assignments based on specific learning objectives and several trials (with accompanying errors along the way) spread over multiple semesters.

What has not come out of any of these efforts—individual or collaborative—is a consensus about what we know, as opposed to what we hope or suspect, about the real impact of technology on student learning. Much more research is needed before such a consensus will emerge.

Still, the very technologies we are experimenting with are expanding our understanding of their utility for teaching our students the liberal arts. So much of what we don't know about student learning is the result of the closed environment of the classroom. The new media, however, have the potential to make teaching and learning transparent.

As scholars we will not accept the results of research that we cannot evaluate for weaknesses, contradictions, or just plain lack of imagination. But as teachers we regularly nod approvingly at colleagues whose student evaluations are strong and who evince a commitment to teaching and learning in our meetings and private conversations. Only rarely do we probe deeper in the way we review a new monograph in our field. Just because our colleagues say they love teaching and their students like them, how do we know that their courses achieved their stated goals? I am not saying that these colleagues are not excellent teachers, nor that their students are not learning. I am simply pointing out that we don't know whether these propositions are true or not.

New information technologies are breaking down the literal and figurative walls that hide our teaching and our students' learning from public view. When students post written work in a threaded discussion forum, it becomes visible to a larger audience, is searchable, and can be analyzed in ways that are all but impossible when that same work is turned in as printed text. And when we respond to our students online, the content of our own critique and support is equally transparent. These new public texts—whether they are in the form of Web sites, hypertexts, online film clips, or other media—offer us opportunities to ask questions about faculty teaching and student learning that were unavailable to us just ten years ago.

As new media open up what is happening in our classrooms, faculty interested in teaching and learning with technology are posing their research questions, charting the progress of that research, proposing conclusions, and ultimately publishing online the results of their inquiries. Examples of this research are available on the Web sites of the Visible Knowledge Project <crossroads.georgetown.edu/vkp/people/>, the University of Nebraska's Peer Review of Teaching project <www.unl.edu/peerrev/>, and the Massachusetts Institute of Technology's OpenCourseWare project <ocw.mit.edu/>. As more faculty offer their teaching up to public scrutiny, their contributions will help us determine just what is and is not happening when we change our curricula to accommodate information technologies.

To be sure, transparency presents risks. Each of us knows a story—true or apocryphal—of a colleague victimized by negative peer teaching evaluations. However, as our teaching becomes more transparent, critics will find it more difficult to make unsubstantiated charges about it. As long as we hide our classrooms from public scrutiny, any tale told about what goes on in them might just be true. But if we allow the world to peek in and poke around, it becomes all but impossible to make up stories about what is and isn't going on in them.

Unanswered Questions

For all these promising developments, we face a challenge from our students that we are ill equipped to address. As they become more adept users of information technologies, they will probably begin to produce new forms of knowledge that cannot be readily assessed by our conventional measures. In my own discipline, we have relied on the narrative for more than 2,000 years to present historical information and argument. New media, especially the emerging tools for networking information, offer new ways to convey that knowledge and to analyze and organize historical content. How will we assess student work developed through these novel means? How will we know if what students create extends our understanding of the past, or merely complicates it?

Today, we have no answer for these questions. Until we do, we will remain on the brink of new forms of liberal learning rather than fully engaged in them. How will we move forward? Right now, funds for the disciplinary-based classroom research that is needed come solely from individual institutions and rarely amount to more than a course buyout. Real scholarship—that which significantly advances our understanding of complex problems—does not happen when a faculty member teaches one fewer course. That kind of research happens when a scholar takes a semester (or a year) away from his other duties and devotes all of his intellectual resources to the problem at hand.

Across the country, colleges and universities are installing the wireless Web and completing the technology infrastructure on their campuses. We would be better served, however, if our institutions spent some of the scarce funds they are devoting to these goals on research into how the good old wired Web influences student learning and how that new infrastructure can best be used. If we do not find funding for this research soon, we will end up with instruction in general education that is technologically advanced while we are left wondering whether real learning is actually happening.

College Lectures Go Digital

By Kimberly Marselas
The (Annapolis, MD) *Capital*, December 3, 2005

Those tiny white headphones are nearly ubiquitous. All over college campuses, the cords of the trademark iPod accessories burrow into countless hooded sweatshirts

Handheld digital music players are so mainstream these days that many professors are bringing them into the classroom, too. After all, Apple's trendy iPods and other MP3 players don't just play music. They can hold photos, video and record songs, lectures or just about anything else—and that provides a new way to reach out to students.

At Anne Arundel Community College, several instructors are experimenting with digital recordings this fall, and school officials are finalizing plans to make those recordings available online.

"We're at the very, very early stages of podcasting," said professor Shad Ewart, director of business programs for the Arnold school.

Though Mr. Ewart is recording his lectures from his Principles of Accounting I class, they've yet to go live on the Internet. That's largely because administrators are still deciding whether the general public should have access to classroom material or whether recorded lectures should be posted on a password-protected site.

Even as they work out the details, college officials held a Web conference Wednesday designed to encourage faculty to use podcasting as a teaching tool. With the latest incarnation of the iPod, even videocasting is an option now.

Local educators want to make sure that even those who aren't crazy about the new technology can keep pace with the evolution.

"You get the early adopters in on it and then it kind of diffuses out to the rest of the faculty," said Paul Warner, director of learning technologies at AACC. "There's really this whole convergence of technology upon us now."

How It Works

After recording a lecture or sound bites, professors transfer the material from their iPods or other MP3 players to a computer. There, they can convert it to a smaller file using a program such as Audacity, and post it on a Web site or e-mail it directly to students.

Students can listen to the material in a variety of formats, and some schools lend out iPods or other players to students who don't have their own. Duke University led the way with the iPod First-Year Experience in August 2004. The private university in Durham, N.C., gave iPods and voice recorders to 1,600 incoming freshmen, who used them in foreign language, humanities and computational methods courses.

> *The goal of podcasting is to make lectures portable, but it also allows for repetition and reinforcement.*

Universities from Georgia to Minnesota followed, either by distributing iPods to their students or encouraging professors to podcast.

Some professors worry that access to podcast files would be an issue for students without their own MP3 players, and University of Maryland junior Megan Carroll agreed that iPods only seem like they're everywhere.

"I know a lot of people who don't have iPods" said the Arundel High School graduate, who got her audio-only iPod mini in September. "And they're kind of expensive."

Although Apple's latest model starts at $299, AACC's Mr. Ewart expects access won't be a much of a problem on his campus. Students will ultimately be able to download files on school computers, but he thinks most will want to zap files to their own players.

"From what I've noticed, they've all got them in their ears," he said. "If it's not an iPod, it's some other type of MP3 player."

The goal of podcasting is to make lectures portable, but it also allows for repetition and reinforcement—a major plus when classroom time is limited.

"The first time a student hears something is not necessarily when it sinks in," said Dr. Patrick Jackson, a self-described tech geek and assistant professor of international relations at American University's School of International Service. "By recording these and making them available as MP3s, they can actually get what you're saying."

Dr. Jackson uses an iPod in courses covering theory, research methodology and the philosophy of social science. He said the "hip factor" of the technology allows teachers to connect with their students, but it also has practical applications.

"iPods are very cool," he announced during a recent faculty forum on digital audio at the University of Maryland, College Park. "Now how can we use them to fulfill some of the basic foundations we're supposed to as university professors?"

For starters, Dr. Jackson says sending lectures or clips from other sources to students via the Internet allows him to devote more class time to informed discussions, readings and one-on-one student assistance. He finds that allowing students to decide how they'll listen to a file—at the computer, downloaded on their own iPod or burned to CD—and where—at their desk, at the gym or in the car—gets them more excited about learning.

He's found that most important for students who are just learning English. While they may not stop a professor to repeat something during class, they are in control when listening to a podcast. The student can slow down a lecture, repeat it multiple times and skip over parts he or she understood initially.

Mr. Ewart has been recorded on cassette tape for years by students with limited English proficiency and said the podcasting craze is only the latest incarnation of that study aid.

He thinks iPods have the potential to help traditional adult community college students as well. They may have to choose between attending a class, going to work or staying home to care for a sick child. In those cases, a podcast offers a good backup.

Mr. Ewart isn't concerned, however, that students will intentionally skip classes knowing they have audio files to rely on.

"I don't think it's an incentive not to come to class," he said, adding that accounting courses require incremental skills that aren't easily acquired by listening to lectures over the Internet the night before an exam.

Branching Out

The Naval Academy and St. John's College aren't jumping on the podcast bandwagon just yet. At St. John's, where classes are discussion-based, lectures don't exist and professors have been replaced by tutors, student leaders say it would take a radical transformation for podcasts to catch on.

"It would never be used as part of our instruction because you can't have a conversation with an iPod," said Chris Aamot, St. John's director of student services, who thinks podcasting is a passing fad. "People have learned based on talking to each other for thousands of years. No matter what the technology, it's not a person."

But, as other area schools begin to embrace iPods, St. John's may find itself in the minority.

Jo Paoletti, director of undergraduate studies for Maryland's American Studies Department, said next year's introductory course will include weekly podcasts with a "radio show format" that includes interviews, short lectures and broadcasts from association meetings.

Arabic instructor Ridha Krizi said the university's School of Languages, Literature and Cultures also issued iPods to 11 students last year, allowing them to listen to lessons and record verbal practice and feedback for their professors.

"I hope this is only the beginning of what we can do," he said.

Bringing Blogs into the Classroom

"New Media" Platform Gaining Steam at Universities

By Patrick Beeson
Quill, August 1, 2005

University of Alabama senior Christine Green couldn't describe what a Web log was before the first day of her opinion writing class. But she had to learn fast. After all, her grade depended on it.

"Almost all of my friends don't know what a blog is," Green said. "It had been maybe two months before (the class started) that I knew what blogs were."

Green, who is majoring in economics and journalism, was better off than many of the 13 other students taking the somewhat experimental course—the first in the university's journalism program to require the use of Web logs, or online journals of brief chronological entries commonly called "blogs."

But the idea of using blogs to teach journalism opinion writing at UA almost didn't happen. In fact, it was such a last-minute addition that instructor Carolyn Mason couldn't add it to the class syllabus.

"I knew as little as they did at first," Mason said. "Their initial reaction, with a few exceptions, was 'what's a blog?'"

The difficulty in explaining the concept of blogging as it relates to journalism was probably not a surprise given its association with "new media," which not every university journalism program has adopted yet. However, the recent push by maverick journalism instructors like Mason is helping reveal innovative teaching methods for the now-popular Internet publishing form, including getting students used to public scrutiny.

It's also becoming a way to bridge the increasing gap to young students more familiar with reading the news on a computer screen than an inked sheet of paper. These news consumers ages 18 to 34 said the Internet, by a 41-to-15 percent margin over second-ranked local TV, is "the most useful way to learn," according to a May 2004 Frank N. Magid Associates survey conducted for the Carnegie Corporation.

Students in Mason's opinion writing class created their blogs using Google's blogging tool, Blogger.com. All of the blogs were then put under the umbrella of Mason's blog and linked together to form a virtual classroom.

Grades were earned for participation, good writing, regular updates—at least once per week—and for posting assignments. Mason also used the blog to communicate with the class after hours with links to suggested readings.

"I was looking for a way to showcase students' work," she said. "(Blogs were) perfect for opinion writing class."

Mason also was intrigued with how a group blog could add to an editorial team atmosphere common in the workplace, but not so common in college classrooms. Students could read their class-mates' work and overcome shyness about their opinion writing.

"This forced them to put it out there," she said.

Rachel Telehany, a UA senior majoring in journalism, is plan-ning to enter the school's graduate program in the fall. She said adding a form of publishing in the class also brought an element of professionalism.

"It was an experiment, but I think it worked," Telehany said.

The huge peer pressure brought on by the blogs made many stu-

---

"I was looking for a way to showcase students' work. (Blogs were) perfect for opinion writing class."—Carolyn Mason, an instructor at the University of Alabama

---

dents take extra care in editing their articles prior to posting. In the past, students simply turned in assignments to the instructor.

It also added a sense of camaraderie to the class.

"They really support each other even though their opinions are widely diverse," Mason said. "There's a group closeness and com-passion I've never seen in all my years of teaching.

"I can only figure that it's from the blog."

Blogging Core Journalism Courses

Despite the recent mainstream media blitz on blogs, they actu-ally have been used in journalism programs since their widespread introduction in 1999. Since that time, blogs have jumped from the "new media" niche to the syllabi of core classes.

The University of Southern California's Annenberg School for Communication began its use of blogs in the school's online jour-nalism course in fall 1999. Assistant professor of journalism Larry Pryor taught that class, whose blog, rolled on the school's Online Journalism Review Web site, avoided quirky, individualized voices for a more refined sound.

Pryor said that since its inception, the design and name of the blog, "News Blog," has taken the format of other blogs on the Web.

"(The blog) didn't do that before. (We) called them news briefs," he said.

The blog's content also consists of both mainstream media and blog coverage. The latter wasn't addressed until the past few semesters.

"Sort of an evolutionary thing," he said. "Our coverage reflects that."

The students working on the News Blog mostly are freshman and sophomore journalism majors. Paid graduate students edit the content, which gets wide, daily exposure to a variety of audiences including professional journalists, newspaper executives and government officials.

Each post to the blog is 60 to 200 words with a headline of five to 10 words. Students writing the posts are taught to paraphrase the original story, selecting key facts and notable quotes.

Pryor said the blogs are part of the learning experience for student journalists. He said it helps make their writing more concise and focused, while also examining how blogging relates to traditional journalism.

"The only real issue is getting [students] familiar with the idea that this is going to be read by other people."—Robert Niles, editor of *Online Journalism Review*

"It's forced them to confront these questions associated with blogging," he said.

Robert Niles, editor of the *Online Journalism Review*, helped push USC's Internet news briefs into the News Blog format after becoming an adjunct faculty member in fall 2003. He teaches online reporting, newswriting and computer assisted reporting courses at the university.

Niles said the primary advantage to beginning journalism students writing blogs is the transition from stilted, academic writing to journalistic writing, while working on accuracy and focus. He compares blogs to writing journals, a common exercise for core journalism courses.

"Students are more natural," he said. "At least they've dropped this dry, academic tone that they've brought to class."

Most journalism students in Niles' classes know about blogs, but many don't realize the extent of their Internet audience.

"The only real issue is getting them familiar with the idea that this is going to be read by other people," he said. "Conceivably, your parents could be reading this (the blog). That usually takes a week or two to figure out."

Other Uses for Instruction

While USC blazes a path in the use of blogs in core college journalism courses, other schools are just leaving the trailhead. But technology-savvy students at either end appear to be adapting without many problems.

Leslie-Jean Thornton, a journalism instructor at Arizona State University's Cronkite School of Journalism and Mass Communications, teaches online media and advanced editing courses, both using blogs. That semester was Thornton's first attempt in using the publishing form in the classroom.

Though Thornton's two classes use blogs only for discussion, rather than a true publishing outlet, she still believes it gives students a more realistic view of the profession. It also seems to be more in tune with the younger generation's way of thinking.

"In general we're just tending to become a more online, computer literate society," she said. "(We want to get) the challenge and excitement that other bloggers feel."

Journalism students at Washington and Lee University in Lexington, Va., are getting a similar taste of blogs without actually entering the growing community of bloggers or what's being called the "blogosphere."

Associate professor of journalism Claudette Artwick teaches the course "Digital Journalism and Society" where blogs are discussed in terms of journalism and democracy. Though students don't post to a blog, they do read, analyze and discuss them.

Artwick said studying blogs enhances students' understanding of journalism. She said blog-related issues are timely and relevant to journalistic issues.

"By asking if bloggers are journalists, students re-examine what a journalist is and if or how a blogger fits in that role," she said.

Yet, other professors of journalism, some with a more cynical perspective of blogs, are praising the popular publishing form for its ability to enliven students' interest in journalism.

University of North Carolina associate professor of journalism Debashis "Deb" Aikat is one of those cynics about the attention mainstream media are giving to blogs. He even refers to blogs as "a glorified bulletin board" rather than a source for original content.

"It's like a DJ in a music show. The DJ doesn't create the music but picks from a list," Aikat said.

Despite his feelings about the blog hype, Aikat requires students taking his "Global Impact of New Communication Technologies" course to create a blog using the Blogger.com tools. Students then pick a global issue, construct a focus and post blog rolls. All of these steps are positioned into "bite-sized chunks" for students.

Aikat said the global reach of the Internet and blogs was perfect for a course on global communication.

"It's a very vibrant electronic community that would otherwise be limited by geography," he said. "This is a wonderful thing."

But one of the most gratifying aspects of using blogs to teach a journalism course for Aikat was that it took the professor out from behind the podium. He is a participant instead of a fountain head.

"It made discussion very rich," he said. "Students thought it was cool that they could create a blog."

Full Integration

Blogs in university journalism programs are still limited largely by their use in only one or two of the total classes being offered. Some schools, mostly graduate programs, are bucking this approach to merge blogs into almost every course.

In fall 2002, University of California Berkeley's Graduate School of Journalism took an experimental leap into the blogosphere with blPblog. John Battelle, a recent teaching fellow and co-founder of *WIRED* magazine, and Paul Grabowicz, assistant dean, adjunct professor and director of the school's new media program, decided to use blogs to report on the issue of intellectual property. This small class with a handful of students would eventually spawn one of the most expansive collegiate journalism blogging efforts in the nation.

UC Berkeley's blogs are contained on the school of journalism's "North Gate" Web site. They encompass everything from the war on terror, news from China, last year's presidential election, issues in traq and hate crimes in the town of Davis, Calif.

"It has become standard fare to use blogging software in class," Grabowicz said.

The invitation of public interaction with journalism students is both a challenging and intimidating sidebar for the new media director. But it's this relationship he is trying to instill with the young journalists in order to better prepare them for a profession grounded in the public arena.

"We are moving toward the idea that the Web is an interactive medium," he said. "The blog invites that. It forces the students to think that through. The public isn't a passive recipient."

Grabowicz said that even on the most passive journalistic level, blogs keep students in touch with people reading them. He said the next step is more interaction with those readers.

"If you just have them write, that's all well and good, but the test is when they get the public feedback," he said. "The bridge between what a student journalist does and what a professional does is publishing.

"It's not playtime any more."

University Class Blogs

Many universities and schools of journalism are either using or beginning to use blogs to teach journalism. Some, such as UC Berkeley and USC, are more established programs, but others are making headway in their use of blogs in the classroom.

Here are links to those programs' blogs:

University of California Berkeley's intellectual property blog, blP-blog
(http://www.blplog.com/)
The blPblog was created in 2002 as an experimental way to teach the subject of intellectual property and transition into new communication technologies. Though that class has since ended, the blog is being maintained by Mary Hodder, from the university's School of Information and Management Systems.

University of Southern California's Online Journalism Review News Blog
(http:#www.ojr.org/ojr/blog/)
The News Blog on the Online Journalism Review Web site, run by USC's Annenberg School for Communication, is updated daily with news briefs. Each post features content links for additional context on the topic being address.

University of Arizona's "Rimrats" and "Blogglob" blogs
(http:#rimrats.blogspot.com/)
(http:#spring425.blogspot.com/)
The Rimrats and Blogglob blogs used in University of Arizona journalism courses "Advanced Editing 413" and "Online Media 425" reveals how some schools are teaching with blogs. Both use daily posts from professor Leslie-Jean Thornton to point students to online articles, and offer writing and editing tips.

University of Alabama Opinion Writing blog
(http://carolynsopinionclass.blogspot.com/)
Carolyn Mason's opinion writing blog "Everyone has one" is the first such effort for the university's College of Communication and Information Sciences. Mason and her students post online columns and other items of interest, including student work for class discussion.

Digital Archives Are a Gift of Wisdom to Be Used Wisely

By Roy Rosenzweig
The Chronicle of Higher Education, June 24, 2005

"What's the big deal?" was the grumpy question of a fellow participant in a workshop at the Library of Congress in the summer of
1996. The library was showing off its still very new digital archive,
which it had dubbed American Memory. The workshop aimed to
show how the Web-based repository of photographs, documents,
newspapers, films, maps, and sounds could transform teaching. My
colleague, who taught at a major research university, was unper-
suaded. "I'd rather send students to the library," he announced.

But to me, it was a big deal—a very big deal—and the answer to a
problem I had been grappling with for more than 15 years. When I
started teaching as a graduate student in the mid-1970s, I quickly
learned that the best way to excite students about my field, history,
was to involve them directly with the "stuff" of the past—the primary sources—and to show them, by asking them to do it, what it
means to think like a historian. As a graduate-student instructor,
that was pretty easy. After all, I was at another of those big
research institutions (Harvard University) with one of the nation's
greatest libraries. I could "send students to the library," and in a
short walk from their dorms, they could find more primary sources
than they could exhaust in a lifetime.

When I arrived at George Mason University in the fall of 1981 as
an assistant professor, things suddenly became much harder. We
had a very modest library in those days. And more problematic from
the perspective of a 19th- and 20-century American historian, it was
a very new library, with relatively few old books, journals, and magazines. I could "send students to the library," but they would not
find the rich bodies of primary sources that Harvard had in abundance. A simple assignment asking them to compare advertisements in two popular magazines of the 1920s was out of the
question, especially in an evening section of my survey course, filled
with students who could not journey to more-distant libraries
because of full-time jobs and family responsibilities.

I now know that my experience was not unique but was shared by scholars in many different fields, at many different institutions. Since then, however, much has changed in the world of Web-based teaching: We have an array of new opportunities, but we also have new limitations that we haven't yet confronted.

I spent a lot of time in the 1980s devising less-than-satisfactory strategies to work around the constraints—photocopying piles of documents myself and putting them on reserve, for example. But in the latter part of the decade, I began to glimpse a solution. I read in computer magazines about this new thing called the CD-ROM, which could hold thousands of pages of text as well as photographs, sound files, and (later) moving pictures. In the early 1990s, I joined with my friends Stephen Brier and Joshua Brown at the American Social History Project, based at the Graduate Center of the City University of New York, to produce, with the help of the Voyager Company, such a disk. When *Who Built America?* appeared in 1993, we promoted it with an enthusiasm that now seems quaint. We would hold up the silvery, thin disk and exclaim (often to incredulous audiences) that it contained: Five thousand pages of text! Seven hundred images! Four hours of oral history, music, and speeches! Forty-five minutes of film!

Actually, our enthusiasm was already becoming dated in 1993. That year brought a much more momentous development for the future of technology and teaching than the publication of our CD-ROM—the appearance of Mosaic, the first easy-to-use graphic Web browser that ran on most standard computers. Between mid-1993 and mid-1995, the number of Web servers—the computers that house Web sites—jumped from 130 to 22,000.

Progress in the last 10 years has been nothing short of astonishing. The Library of Congress's American Memory project now presents more than nine million historical documents. The New York Public Library's Digital Gallery contains more than 300,000 images digitized from its extraordinary collections. PictureAustralia presents 770,000 images from 28 cultural agencies in that country; the International Dunhuang Project, a cross-national collaboration, serves up 100,000 digitized images of artifacts, manuscripts, and paintings from the trade routes of the Silk Road. Most dramatically, the search-engine behemoth Google has announced plans to digitize at least 15 million books. Hundreds of millions of federal, foundation, and corporate dollars have already gone into digitizing a startlingly large proportion of our cultural heritage, and more is to come.

That is about as dramatic a development in access to cultural resources in a single decade as any of us are likely to see in our lifetimes, and it has opened up enormously exciting possibilities for teachers not just of American history and culture but in numerous disciplines that have experienced similar transformations. To be sure, not everything will become digital (nor should it), but where we instructors once struggled with the scarcity of documents for our students to use, we now participate in what John F. McClymer, a historian at Assumption College, calls a "pedagogy of abundance." The developments in history are broadly illustrative of both the possibilities and the problems of that pedagogy.

Has the new abundance of electronic resources solved all our difficulties as teachers? Can we now just "send students to the Web?" Most scholars and teachers would answer "no," immediately starting to talk about the vast quantities of junk out there on the Web. I disagree. The quality of Web-based historical resources is surprisingly good and getting better. My concern is not that students will find junk online, but rather that they will fail to gain full access to the Web's riches or won't know what do with those riches when they find them.

> *[The Web] offers a much less controlled environment than libraries, whose collections have been shaped by generations of professionals.*

Complaints about the low quality of the Web's resources were loudest in its early days. Just look to the pages of *The Chronicle*. In a November 1996 essay, a well-known historian proclaimed herself "disturbed by some aspects of . . . the new technology's impact on learning and scholarship." "Like postmodernism," Gertrude Himmelfarb complained, "the Internet does not distinguish between the true and the false, the important and the trivial, the enduring and the ephemeral." Internet search engines, she said, "will produce a comic strip or advertising slogan as readily as a quotation from the Bible or Shakespeare." Himmelfarb was right to sense danger out on the Web—it offers a much less controlled environment than libraries, whose collections have been shaped by generations of professionals—and her worries have been regularly echoed by other scholars.

Yet like a living organism, the Web has developed two remarkable, if imperfect, sets of mechanisms for healing its defects.

The first are the automated approaches that have made the founders of Google billionaires. Himmelfarb was not the only person to notice the inadequacy of search engines in 1996. That year, two Stanford computer-science students, Lawrence Page and Sergey Brin, began building BackRub, a new search engine named for its then-unique capacity to analyze the "back links" to Web sites. Within two years, BackRub became Google, and its use of link analysis (and some other magic) to roughly rank the reputation of sites transformed Web searching.

Google's ranking system has its limitations. The Hitler Historical Museum's site, which takes an "unbiased" (i.e., uncritical) view of the German leader, shows up in the first 10 results for a search on "Adolf Hitler." But the rankings do go some distance toward separating the wheat from the chaff. You can find the Holocaust deniers at the Institute for Historical Review on the Web, but not in the first 100 hits on Google (or Yahoo) if you search on "holocaust"; that may be because few reputable sites link to the so-called institute.

Perhaps less well recognized is that the same algorithmic procedures behind Google, combined with the direct access that the company (as well as Yahoo) offers to its data, open up more-advanced possibilities for sorting out good and bad information mathematically. For example, Dan Cohen, my colleague at the Center for History and New Media at George Mason, has developed H-Bot, the Automated Historical Fact Finder, which can answer historical questions like "When did Charles Darwin publish *The Origin of Species?*" with a surprising degree of accuracy, simply by querying Google and analyzing the results statistically.

But even the most refined statistical and mathematical tools are unlikely to be able to make the kind of qualitative judgments historians often need to make. A second set of more social mechanisms—nascent forms of peer review—help keep students away from the bogus documents and poor-quality archives they will inevitably encounter online. Just as the Web has spawned plenty of problematic history Web sites, it has also provided a platform for dozens of Web resources with the goal of steering people away from those sites. For example, Thomas Daccord, a high-school teacher at Noble & Greenough School, in Dedham, Mass., has created Best of History Web Sites. History Matters: The U.S. Survey Course on the Web (developed by the social-history project at CUNY and the new-media center at George Mason) annotates the 850 best Web sites in American history; a sibling, World History Matters, at George Mason, has begun to do the same in that field.

Even more interesting is a kind of spontaneous review process generated by the mass of people on the Web. About four years ago, I stumbled across an interesting online historical "document"—an 1829 letter to President Andrew Jackson from Martin Van Buren, then governor of New York, warning of the threat that a new technology, the railroad, posed to the old technology of canals, and urging the federal government to intervene to "preserve the canals." Van Buren's worries sound suspicious to most American historians. After all, Van Buren opposed federal intervention in the economy. Yet, at least when I checked in early 2001, the document was presented credulously all over the Web. Libertarians at Citizens for a Sound Economy reproduced it to show how stupid politicians often pigheadedly refuse to allow "the market to work unimpeded by regulatory constraints." The former president of the Federal Reserve Bank of Dallas (and now chancellor of the Texas A&M University System) used it in a speech that is posted online to chastise the "window breakers in Seattle" opposed to free trade.

But try entering "van buren canals andrew jackson railroads" in Google today. Your first hit is the snopes.com "urban legends" page, which provides a detailed discussion of why the document is a fraud. Even the libertarians have gotten the message. Two readers of the sound-economy site have used the article's comment feature to warn that the document is a fake. The same collaborative mechanisms of review—applied more systematically—have made the collectively produced and open-source encyclopedia Wikipedia a surprisingly credible resource for historical facts.

If the Web has become a less dangerous place for students to venture, however, it has also become a considerably more expensive arena, and that poses a much more serious problem for those who want to teach with primary sources. It is hard to remember that, but a decade ago, the Web was largely a noncommercial world. It was only in 1995 that dot-com domains came to dominate over dot-edu addresses. Commercialization has had its impact on what we call the History Web, the online repository of digital primary and secondary sources. In fact, some of the most interesting and exciting of those sources are commercial products, often very costly ones, from giant information conglomerates.

For example, the Thomson Corporation offers Eighteenth Century Collections Online, which includes "every significant English-language and foreign-language title printed in Great Britain during the 18th century"—33 million text-searchable pages and nearly 150,000 titles. "We own the 18th century," a Thomson official boasts. Those who want their own share must pay handsomely. A university with 18,000 students can spend more than half a million dollars to acquire the full collection, depending on discounts it receives and other pricing factors. Another extraordinary digital collection, ProQuest Historical Newspapers, contains the full runs of a number of major newspapers. One of my colleagues uses it for weekly primary-source assignments that I could only have dreamed about back in 1981. But a typical university will have to shell out the equivalent of an assistant professor's salary each year to pay for those digital newspapers.

It seems churlish to complain about extraordinary resources that greatly enrich the possibilities for online research and teaching. Surely Thomson, ProQuest, and other businesses are entitled to recoup their multimillion-dollar investments in digitizing the past. But it still needs to be observed that not every college can pay the entry fee to this new digital world. Some may have to decide whether it is more important to have extraordinary digital resources or people to teach about them.

Thus we are in danger of reproducing the information divide of yesterday—where the richest universities with the biggest physical libraries could offer students far better access to materials than other institutions. Of course there are powerful counters to commercialization, especially the support that public agencies and private foundations have provided for digitization and "open content," as well as the eclectic and energetic efforts of enthusiasts and scholars who continue to post primary sources out of a passion for their fields.

But even when students have equal access to online resources, they do not necessarily have equal ability to make effective use of the new, global resource. For many students, the abundance of primary sources can be more puzzling and disorienting than liberating and enlightening. Sam Wineburg, a cognitive psychologist who teaches at Stanford's School of Education, has spent 20 years observing classrooms and talking with both teachers and students about how students read (and misread) historical sources. As his research shows, instructors commonly overstate their ability to analyze primary sources, failing to recognize the challenges that thwart understanding.

In my field, what do students make of the tens of thousands of photographs from the Farm Security Administration put online by the Library of Congress? Most often they see such powerful sources as transparent reflections of a historical "reality"; not, as a historian would, as imperfect refractions—ideological statements by reform-minded photographers who wanted to expose the poverty brought on by the Great Depression and advance the programs of

> *Even when students have equal access to online resources, they do not necessarily have equal ability to make effective use of the new, global resource.*

the New Deal. In the resonant phrase of Randy Bass, a professor of English at Georgetown University and director of the university's Center for New Designs in Learning and Scholarship, the Web has for the first time put "the novice in the archive," giving access to people who were previously barred by the time and expense of getting to archives, or by the entrance requirements imposed by such collections. But still novices lack the skills for critically evaluating primary sources.

Thus far we have done much better at democratizing access to resources than at providing the kind of instruction that would give meaning to those resources. Hundreds of millions of dollars have gone into digitizing historical resources; the money devoted to using the Web to teach students the kinds of historical procedures that trained historians make part of their routine can be measured in the hundreds of thousands of dollars.

Still, there are some promising beginnings. Picturing Modern America 1880–1920, from the Center for Children and Technology, based in New York, offers some thoughtful "historical thinking exercises" for students that, for example, take them step by step through "reading" a photograph—first posing a question, then looking closely and gathering clues, and finally drawing conclusions. Our own History Matters and World History Matters provide guides to "making sense of evidence," as well as illustrations of "scholars in action," in which we show historians analyzing, for instance, a blues song, a Colonial newspaper, or a Thomas Nast cartoon.

In a new project that we have begun in collaboration with Wineburg and his colleagues at Stanford, with the support of the William and Flora Hewlett Foundation, we are building on those approaches on a site that we are calling Historical Thinking Matters. The site, which we will launch in 2006, will, for example, use video clips to model historical thinking; it will use pop-ups and other programming to scaffold primary sources in a way that encourages students to check sources, corroborate evidence, and contextualize it.

For the moment, the danger for students venturing onto the Web is not that they will find either bogus letters or comic strips, but that they won't know how to "read" the vast number of valuable primary sources that they find. It remains to be seen whether we can create useful online aids that not only make information available, but assist users in learning to discriminate and analyze that information.

The larger lesson here is one that we should have learned over and over again in confronting new technology. The most difficult issues are economic, social, and cultural, not technological. The Web has given us a great gift—an unparalleled global digital library and archive that is growing bigger every day. Our task now is to make sure that it remains accessible to all, and to turn the novices we have admitted to it into experts who can use it with intelligence and thoughtfulness. If we can succeed not just in democratizing access to materials like online historical evidence but also in helping students make sense of that evidence, that will be a very big deal.

Electronic Archives for Academe

The following are listed in the order in which they are discussed in the accompanying article:

American Memory
http://memory.loc.gov/ammem
Web-based repository of photographs, documents, newspapers, films, and maps from the Library of Congress.

PictureAustralia
http://www.pictureaustralia.org/newsarchive.html
770,000 images from 28 cultural agencies in Australia.

International Dunhuang Project
http://idp.bl.uk
A cross-national collaboration with 100,000 images of artifacts, manuscripts, and paintings from the trade routes of the Silk Road.

H-Bot, the Automated Historical Fact Finder
http://chnm.gmu.edu/tools/h-bot
Automated answers to historical questions.

Best of History Web Sites
http://www.besthistorysites.net/about.shtml
A guide created by Thomas Daccord, a teacher at Noble & Greenough School, in Dedham, Mass., to more than 1,000 sites.

History Matters: The U.S. Survey Course on the Web
http://historymatters.gmu.edu/expansion.html
Annotates 850 Web sites in American history.

World History Matters
http://chnm.gmu.edu/worldhistorymatters
A sibling to the History Matters site.

Eighteenth Century Collections Online
http://www.gale.com/EighteenthCentury

Includes "every significant English-language and foreign-language title printed in Great Britain during the 18th century," according to the publisher. Charges substantial fees to libraries.

ProQuest Historical Newspapers
http://www.il.proquest.com/products/pt-product-HistNews.shtml
Full runs of a number of major newspapers. Substantial fees to libraries.

Picturing Modern America 1880–1920
http://www.edc.org/CCT/PMA/
Thoughtful "historical thinking exercises" for students from the Center for Children and Technology, based in New York.

Classic Lit Goes Txt Msging

By Shelley Emling
Cox News Service, November 21, 2005

2B? NT2B? = ???

It might look like pure gibberish but it's pure literature—at least as pure as literature can be when expressed as a text message.

Dot Mobile, a British cellphone service for students, has devised a program that will offer concise summaries of classic works of literature in text-message format. The new service has been designed to act as a review tool for students about to take exams on literature.

Initially the cell plan will send major quotations and plot summaries from at least seven classics, including Shakespeare's "Romeo and Juliet," Jane Austen's "Pride and Prejudice" and William Golding's "Lord of the Flies," to cellphones to act as a reminder for students.

Dot Mobile plans to make the complete works of Shakespeare and Geoffrey Chaucer's "The Canterbury Tales" available in text form in April.

Dot Mobile contracted the services of John Sutherland, an English professor at University College London, in developing the plan.

"The educational opportunities it offers are immense," Sutherland said. ". . . You could shrink the whole five-act text of 'Hamlet' into a few thousand characters. And those few thousand characters could serve as a memory aide, enabling you to back-translate into the golden syllables of the original."

Those golden syllables are fine the way they are, say some literary purists.

Helen Hackett, a literature expert at University College London, said the service sounds like little but a commercial gimmick.

"You can't read a book without reading the book," Hackett said. "Students may be able to get plot summaries from their mobiles, but this won't get them very far in preparing for exams at degree level.

"The students who do well are the ones who love the language of literature, and love to write well themselves," she said. "Text message summaries have nothing to offer for this purpose."

But Sutherland believes that even Shakespeare would have approved of the abbreviated versions.

"While some may argue that Dickens is really too big a morsel to be swallowed by text, the 'Great Inimitable' himself began working life as a shorthand writer and he would, I suspect, have approved of the brevity if nothing else," he said.

Dot Mobile spokesman Steven Brabenec said the service would help thousands of students remember key plots and quotes. But he emphasized that it won't be used to help students cheat, since universities have long barred cellphones from exam halls.

Text messaging—a form of e-mail for the phone—took off much faster in Europe and in Asia than in the United States. This year more than 32 billion text messages will be sent in Britain alone, compared with 26 billion in 2004, according to the Mobile Data Association.

In China, the more than 383 million cellphone subscribers (up 48 million from last year) sent 246 billion text messages in the first 10 months of this year, the Ministry of Information said last week.

Rob Enderle, principal analyst at the California technology research firm Enderle Group, said that the Dot Mobile plan is a harbinger of the future—even in the United States.

"Generally schools have been trying to eliminate phone use because they consider it cheating," he said. "But the future will be defined by kids who know how best to use these tools as we increasingly create a symbiotic relationship with technology."

"This is an indicator that schools are beginning to embrace this change," he said.

The turning of great texts into text isn't exactly new.

In September, the Bible Society of Australia converted all 31,173 verses of the Bible into text-speak beginning with "In da bginnin God cre8d da heavens & da earth."

Examples of classic text available from Dot Mobile for college students:

"A horse, a horse, my kingdom for a horse." (Shakespeare, *Richard III*): Ahors,, m'kndgdom 4 Ahors

"Tomorrow and tomorrow and tomorrow." (Shakespeare, *Macbeth*): 2morrow & &

"Whenever you feel like criticizing anyone . . . just remember that all the people in this world haven't had the advantages that you've had." (F. Scott Fitzgerald, *The Great Gatsby*): WenevaUFeelLykDissinNe1,jstMemba-DatAlDaPplnDaWrldHvntHdDaVantgsUvAd

"If you really want to hear about it, the first thing you'll probably want to know is where I was born, and what my lousy childhood was like, and how my parents were occupied and all before they had me, and all that David Copperfield kind of crap, but I don't feel like going into it, if you want to know the truth." (J.D. Salinger, *The Catcher in the Rye*): IfURlyWnt2HrBout-It,Da1stFingUlProbWnt2NoIsWherIWsBorn&WotMyLousyChldhdWs-Lyk&HwMyRentsWerOcupyd&AlB4TheyHdMe&AlThtDaveCopafieldKin-daCr"p,BtIDnFeelLykGoinIntaItIfUWannaNoDaTruf

Snd yr ntrE!

V. New Media Communities and Their Discontents

Editor's Introduction

Perhaps the greatest development facilitated by the new media is the virtual community—groups of people who form connections on the Internet rather than in person. Without such communities, many of the innovations that gave rise to the new media would never have been possible. The success of blogs or Web-based political campaigning, for instance, is in many ways dependent upon the participation of numerous people who are unlikely to meet each other face to face, whether such participation involves a number of people contributing to a single Web site or a number of blog writers' developing relationships on the Net. Indeed, the value of blogs as news, as we saw in this book's first and second chapters, is often a consequence of the bloggers' participating in a community, which performs, among other things, the role of fact checker. This section explores other types of Web communities, those that use technology as a means of personal as well as mass communication.

The first two articles take a look at social Web sites. Patrick Verel's "Weaving the Web" focuses on social networking—"a term coined," Verel explains, "to describe the phenomenon of people connecting to friends, family and colleagues through the World Wide Web." The article discusses how sites such as Friendster and MySpace are being used to form and maintain relationships and draws attention to the other benefits of these Web sites, briefly exploring how they are being used to promote musical groups. Marco R. della Cava's "Utopia Goes Digital" examines the convergence of video-game technology and social-networking Web sites, a phenomenon that has allowed users to create alternative lives in virtual worlds away from the annoyances and difficulties of real life. Such sites, della Cava goes on to argue, belie "the accusation that technology alienates humans from each other." Second Life, the virtual world that is della Cava's primary focus, has even begun to provide outlets for those suffering from such disorders as Asperger's syndrome, a form of autism, that make socializing nearly impossible. "The community," he reveals, "is used by two dozen adults with Asperger's syndrome to work on social skills without having to interact face-to-face."

With Ellen Lee's examination of the wiki, a community-based publishing system, the chapter shifts its focus from Web sites formed in order to build communities to Web sites that rely upon a community forming around them to achieve a particular goal. Inspired by Wikipedia, the online, user-created encyclopedia predicated on the idea that "One know-it-all is not enough; more is better," wikis have proliferated over the last few years. "Unlike other Web sites created and managed by a single person or entity, wikis are truly for the people, by the people," Lee writes. That, some say, is often the problem, especially because their purpose is to produce fact-based publications: No one can be certain that those contributing to the publication are knowledgeable

139

enough to achieve accuracy. Advocates counter that wikis provide readers the opportunity to correct factual errors, whereas when a mistake appears in print, it must stand until another edition of the book is published, and even then, the old edition remains in circulation.

While community formation is an important part of Internet life, it is not the only part. People flock to the Web to escape the pressures associated with belonging to communities, and Web-based technologies are also satisfying the impulse to escape. Bob Tedeschi's "To Internet Stores, It's All About the Personal Touch" discusses Web sites that take advantage of such technologies. By exploiting the methods of mass production, upstart companies, Tedeschi explains, are developing Internet stores—CafePress.com and Zazzle, for example—that enable users to develop, purchase, and/or sell custom-designed items at affordable prices. These stores enable individuals to avoid, in small ways at least, the conformity bred by a retail industry that tries to dictate fashion trends. Now anyone can design his or her own look with the click of a few buttons, purchase the creation, or market it. The trend, these companies say, is growing in popularity and profitability, giving them the ability to "take on Wal-Mart Stores, the world's biggest company."

A book on new media would be incomplete without some discussion of the problems associated with it, and nowhere are these problems more apparent, or more troublesome, than on Internet sites geared toward socializing. Jill King Greenwood's "Authorities Look to Net Predators" discusses how the anonymity of the Web facilitates the activities of criminals, in this case pedophiles, by looking at the problem through the eyes of the authorities attempting to stop it. The book concludes with Victor Gonzales's "Caught in a Spiral of Gaming," an article discussing Internet addiction and the approaches psychiatrists are taking to solve the problem.

Weaving the Web

By Patrick Verel
The Augusta Chronicle (Georgia), March 1, 2005

In the online universe, we're all just a few clicks away from each other.

At least, that's the promise of social networking, a term coined to describe the phenomenon of people connecting to friends, family and colleagues through the World Wide Web.

When Friendster.com, a Mountain View, Calif.–based company, debuted in 2002, it made a splashy entrance as users flocked to the free Web site to browse online profiles. As with online dating sites, member profiles on Friendster feature pictures and lists of favorite movies, music and books. The difference is that, like the Six Degrees of Kevin Bacon game, a user also can see the friends of their friends, or their friends' friends' friends . . . well, you get the idea.

Since Friendster's debut, the number of social networking sites has multiplied, and one newcomer, MySpace.com, is challenging Friendster for supremacy. Other competitors include theface-book.com, which focuses on college students and recent graduates, hi5.com and orkut.com, which is run by the Google search engine.

Matt Grisham, a 24-year-old student at the Medical College of Georgia, recently turned to Friendster to find classmates from his alma mater, Berry College, in Rome, Ga. The Athens, Tenn., native signed up two months ago at the suggestion of a fellow Berry alum.

"Then it was just to procrastinate from studying, just reading about other people and deciding if I wanted to send a message," Mr. Grisham said, laughing.

"I look for something I can relate to in their profile and then message them and just say 'I know how you feel,' or 'I can relate to your situation.' I haven't actually met up with anyone; it's really just bouncing messages back and forth."

Because he's busy with school, Mr. Grisham said, he spends about 10 minutes a day on the site.

"I've enjoyed finding people I haven't seen or spoken to in years, when I really had no idea how to get in touch with them," he said. "We're all split apart, and it makes it easier, because all their schedules are busy."

Dave Wolfe, 34, of Augusta, signed up with Friendster in July to keep in touch with his friend Billy Taylor, who lives in Los Angeles.

"I was pretty skeptical, but there were like thousands of people out there," he said. "Neither of us was actively seeking anything like that, but after taking a look, it seemed pretty cool."

Although he has linked up to 15 friends, Mr. Wolfe views the Web site as more of a diversion than a life-changing innovation. He won't write it off as a fad, though.

"The world is getting to be a smaller place, and I think this is one of the mechanisms that can facilitate that," he said.

It's more useful in Los Angeles, he said, where searching for people with similar interests can yield more results.

"There can be a million people around, and you can still be hanging out with the same 15 people all the time. So it can be a good way to meet new people," Mr. Wolfe said.

> *"The world is getting to be a smaller place, and I think [Friendster] is one of the mechanisms that can facilitate that."*
> —Dave Wolfe, Augusta, GA

That jibes with research conducted by Hitwise, an online-monitoring company that found American Internet users in urban areas are on average 91 percent more likely to visit online social networking sites. The Redwood City, Calif.–based firm also has found that half the visitors to these sites are between 18 and 24 years old. Although dating is a big draw for young people, Friendster Marketing Manager Jeff Roberto said, it's the third-most-popular use amongst the site's 16 million users (a quarter of whom are in the United States). Users of Friendster, he said, tend to skew toward their late 20s, and to keep those users interested, the site recently has added features such as bulletin boards and, most recently, instant messaging.

"Instead of sending an e-mail to a friend and having them forward it for you, you can ping someone in real time and say, 'I know you through so and so,'" Mr. Roberto said.

Josh Martin, 19, signed up for Friendster two years ago with the idea of promoting his band, Estrela.

"It was kind of limited, and then MySpace came out and everyone went onto that," he said. "MySpace is even better because you can put your songs on it, and you can post all the dates you're playing."

MySpace.com began in September 2003 as a music site, where users could listen to snippets of new songs and look up band itineraries. With 150,000 bands on the site, music is still a focus, but it has morphed into much more. Web logs, (or blogs), games, videos, forums and instant messaging have drawn a large audience among 18-to 24-year-olds, and in many circles it has replaced Friendster.

Augusta-area bands Sick Sick Sick, Kill Radius, Hellblinki Sextet and The Josh Pierce Group have a presence on the site, as do clubs The Soul Bar and Sector 7G. A recent search for profiles with pictures within 10 miles of downtown yielded more than 1,000 18-to 30-year-olds.

Mr. Martin used the site to book Estrelas' recent tour from Florida to Tennessee. The only other place on the Web as good for publicizing his band, he said, is livejournal.com

"It was mostly me contacting other bands and seeing if we could play with them," he said "We had a booker, but it all fell through, so it was a last-minute thing. I e-mailed anyone in the area where there were shows and asked if they wanted to let us play with them."

Although he uses it only for promoting his band, Mr. Martin said, MySpace is definitely used for dating and meeting new friends. Among his circle of friends, he has never had to recruit anyone to join.

"Most people are already on it," Mr. Martin said. "MySpace is like a plague."

Utopia Goes Digital

BY MARCO R. DELLA CAVA
USA TODAY, AUGUST 21, 2005

Is the real world grating on you, with its wars, overheated summers and incessant Tom Cruise updates? Just hop online and create a digital you that lives in a utopian cyber-realm. There, you can buy a pixilated house on a lake, go ballooning with like-minded souls and even open up a virtual business that delivers real-world cash.

While you're busy processing that, a few more folks are joining Second Life, a growing adult community—woe to anyone who calls it a game—created by Philip Rosedale, the boyish Bay Area techie at the helm of Linden Lab.

"It's a bit like *The Matrix*," Rosedale says, tapping away at a keyboard as he ushers his avatar—a digital alter ego that can take almost any shape but frequently appears as a buff or buxom humanoid—into Second Life. "We provide the land, and the community builds the actual world, which gives everyone a huge sense of being pioneers in a great experiment."

The appeal of a place like Second Life, a turbocharged version of The Sims, is visceral. It's like being in a hip world that mates *Friends* with *Star Trek*, a global coffee klatch where your custom-designed proxy can make eye contact with humans cloaked in digital finery.

Second Life belies the accusation that technology alienates humans from each other: The community is used by two dozen adults with Asperger's syndrome to work on social skills without having to interact face-to-face.

Using avatars to interact online is a booming trend. It was non-existent a decade ago, but today there are an estimated 5 million subscribers worldwide to dozens of massively multiplayer online games, known as MMOGs. With names like World of Warcraft and EverQuest, most challenge players to reach specified goals, usually with some degree of mayhem and derring-do involved.

But Second Life stands apart in a sea of goal-oriented MMOGs. It has no mission other than the same ones found in real life: Look for a nice place to settle down, build a home, start a business and find fun ways to blow off steam. It is remarkable in its simplistic and, yes, scary ability to provide a way to live a parallel life online.

There also is evidence that once people get a taste of Second Life, they're hooked. Mmogchart.com, which tracks online-game statistics, shows sharp drops in activity among MMOGs with gaming at their core once the game has been mastered. But the trend line for Second Life is a steady march north, evidence that people are not only curious about joining a virtual community to just, well, hang out, but they also stay involved once they get there.

> *This online world already functions much like an authentic community.*

Growing 10% a month since its debut in June 2003, Second Life membership surged 34% in July, to 40,000. "It's still comparatively small now, but I see endless potential," creator Rosedale says. "Realize that 10 million objects have so far been built by our members. I'm stunned by people's endless desire to create."

Although aimed at adults, Second Life isn't neglecting teens. This month, Linden Labs rolled out a teen-oriented version.

Also in play is Finland-born Habbo Hotel, a teen site where Hobbit-like visitors pay to furnish rooms where they can lure fellow Habbos in for a chat or to play a game. Over the past four years, 31 million Habbos have been created in 13 countries, including the USA.

And then there's MTV Networks, which recently paid an estimated $160 million for Neopets, a tween-focused site where children, represented by mystical creatures, play games to help feed their furry friends. About 30 million children have signed up. A Warner Bros. movie is in development.

More of the Worlds

"These virtual worlds will grow," says David Johnson, visiting professor at New York Law School. He helped organize the school's State of Play conferences, which explore the future of online realms.

"Interactions with other people via avatars have an emotionally arresting quality that text-based interactions lack. (These applications) make the idea that there is a real cyberspace quite tangible."

Indeed, this online world already functions much like an authentic community.

Members convened a virtual candlelight vigil last month after the first series of bombings in London, and this weekend they will host an American Cancer Society Relay for Life, in which avatars will walk a course within this world's 122 to-scale square miles and raise real dollars.

If that sounds intriguing, here's what it takes to fly—yes, fly—yourself into Second Life. It starts with buying an avatar for $10. You get a human-looking figure who, at the click of a mouse, is able to soar high above Second Life, the better to decide on an interesting place to alight. Whether it's at a disco or a Vegas-style game room, other avatars can be coaxed into conversation by facing them and typing in a text message. And, if you were wondering, avatars can have sex.

The next level of involvement is buying land at roughly $2 for 512 square meters, which comes with what amounts to a leasing fee—the prime source of Linden Lab's revenue—of $9.95 a month.

Once you're a virtual landowner, you can add anything from stores to homes on your property. You can build them yourself at no cost; everything is painstakingly constructed from "prims," or primitives, that can be manipulated through mouse and keyboard. Or simply buy a ready-built item from someone who has done the work.

At slboutique.com, a beach house goes for 250 Linden dollars (the equivalent of $1); a Learjet costs 600 Linden. Sites such as gamingopenmarket.com and ige.com allow users to exchange real currency for Linden dollars.

Chip Matthews is a freelance artist from Germantown, Md., whose skin (most popular: Mediterranean tone) and clothing for Second Life avatars earn him $1,000 a month.

"Some people have a tough time grasping the concept of people paying for virtual goods," says Matthews, who goes by Chip Midnight online. "But I feel the same way about people spending money on hideous plaid pants for golf."

For many Second Life entrepreneurs, operating a Second Life business "isn't about the money, really, it's about having your imagination returned to you," says Nanci Schenkein, a retired wedding and bar mitzvah planner from Scottsdale, Ariz., whose Second Life persona, Baccara Rhodes, is an in-demand event planner. "You get together with people regardless of age, race or sex and create these amazing things," she says. "But people do think we're nuts."

A Boost for Self-esteem

Online-world creators are banking that this stigma will fade as more homes get wired for high-speed Internet access. "We'll be in position as kids increasingly move from watching TV to interacting with each other on the Web," says Timo Soininen, CEO of interactive game company Sulake, the folks behind Habbo Hotel.

James Horton, 16, of Warrington, England, has seen shy Habbos blossom fast. He likes to lend a hand by volunteering at the hotel's help desk. "People have told me that they're not as confident in their real worlds as they are here," he says.

Second Life serves just such a self-esteem boosting function for a group of residents with Asperger's, a high-functioning form of autism that impairs social interaction.

A year ago, John Lester, director of information technology at Boston's Massachusetts General Hospital, spent $1,000 to buy a private 16-acre island in Second Life that he dubbed Brigadoon.

As creator of the support site braintalk.org, Lester had seen the benefits of having patients interact via e-mail. The more realistic setting of Brigadoon has produced even greater breakthroughs.

"I see them making strong social connections that I'd never seen before," Lester says. "When they're ready, I've asked them to try and leave the island and visit the rest of Second Life."

Which is what creator Rosedale is doing now, soaring past lush hilltops and snowy fields en route to a little fun. But his instantly recognized avatar can't seem to fly two feet without amazed comments popping up in the chat box.

Rosedale flies into a car dealership to check out the goods, then drops in on a bingo-like game called Tringo. Finally, he spots a hot-air balloon and asks for a ride.

As the balloon takes flight, the world below Philip Linden looks eerily familiar, from its misty white sky to its dark blue oceans.

Is this all just a 3-D chat room for lonely hearts? A safe haven for self-expression? A glimpse of the 22nd century? Whatever it is, something is up down there.

"Everything you're seeing now, the community built," Rosedale says as the balloon banks left into a cloud. "It's part of a new weird nation where all bets are off. Here, the future is yours to create."

Real world vs. Second Life

One advantage of living your life online is you get to look mah-velous, thanks to the endless range of body types and fashion apparel at your disposal. Another is that it's much cheaper.

A quick real world vs. Second Life comparison:

	Real world	Second Life
Birth	Earth's hospitals sock you for $5,000 to $8,000, and far more if you arrive by cesarean section.	Linden Lab wants $10 to deliver you into their hands.
Housing	You're a San Francisco success story and want a house that reflects your station in life. That'll cost you seven figures for anything more than a three-bedroom, two-bath starter home.	A cozy beach house in cyberspace will run you 250 Linden dollars, or $1. Add a quaint lion fountain for around 70 cents.
Wheels	Ferraris start around $200,000, and that's once you get up the nerve to walk into the dealership.	A similar virtual ride is $2. Want something funkier to tool around in? How about a Zamboni ice resurfacing machine ($1)?

The Wonderful World of Wikis

By Ellen Lee
Contra Costa Times (California), December 5, 2005

Michele Ann Jenkins and Evan Prodromou were backpacking through Thailand a few years ago when they tried to hunker down for the night at a beach-side place their guide book had recommended.

But when they arrived, they found only the shell of the building. "I knew I wasn't going to be the last person to make this mistake, to follow the guide book to a hotel that didn't exist," Jenkins said. "But there was no way to fix the guide book, to affect the other 10 million copies of the book."

Inspired by Wikipedia, an online encyclopedia that lets anyone contribute, the couple, former Bay Area dotcommers, returned to their home in Montreal and started Wikitravel. The online travel guide—constantly updated, of course—lets anyone chime in on recommendations for places to stay, restaurants to sample and adventures upon which to embark.

Ever since the original Wikipedia launched in 2001, "wikis" have spread all over the Web, illustrating once again how the Internet has transformed the way people get information and the way that information is created.

There are wikis devoted to the possible flu pandemic, *Star Trek* and the Latin-pop singer Shakira. East Bay Democrats used a wiki as a tool to help organize their campaign for presidential candidate John Kerry. Inside some businesses, such as Nokia Corp., employees have begun using wikis to collaborate on company projects.

And wikimania is growing dramatically. In October, 16.3 million people visited Wikipedia, a 267 percent increase from the same month last year, according to Nielsen/NetRatings. Overall, the site has compiled 2.6 million articles in more than 200 languages, including 840,000 in English.

A wiki, from the Hawaiian term for "quick," is an ongoing, ever-evolving, organized compilation of information. Ever wonder how long a cat has been known to live? (Answer: 36 years). Need to learn how to hitchhike through Japan? Chances are that information can be easily found on a wiki and, if not, someone out there is about to add it.

The theory behind wikis is simple: One know-it-all is not enough; more is better. Unlike other Web sites created and managed by a single person or entity, wikis are truly for the people, by the people.

"It's like building a barn," said Colin Jensen, a Fremont software programmer who is part of the Wikitravel community. "You put a window in the barn and once you have it, everybody can use it and enjoy it."

Wikipedia co-founder Jimmy Wales came across the idea as he was trying to create an online encyclopedia. The wiki tool is based on open source technology, which computer programmers have been using for years to develop software jointly through the Internet.

"It's a mass collaboration to build all kinds of things," Wales said. "It's becoming a new model for doing things on the Internet."

Wales' initial project has since expanded to include Wiktionary, Wikiquotes and Wikinews, among others, which are all overseen by the nonprofit parent organization Wikimedia. He also sepa-

---

The theory behind wikis is simple: One know-it-all is not enough; more is better.

---

rately launched a for-profit, advertising-supported company called Wikia, which runs Wikicities. The site hosts wikis for free, allowing fans to make a wiki for their obsessions, from *Star Trek* to *Star Wars* to Shakira.

Dan Carlson, co-founder of Memory Alpha, the *Star Trek* wiki, turned to wiki technology after he found he couldn't keep up with the *Star Trek* database he had spent some 10 years creating. Launched on its own in late 2003, Memory Alpha became part of Wikicities several months ago.

"The idea I latched onto with the wiki concept is you can spread the work around," said the 24-year-old from Delaware. "Everyone can pitch in and go in on their own special interest."

For him, that was *Deep Space Nine* and the *Next Generation* series. "I went in and wrote in-depth articles on the battles featured in *Deep Space Nine*," he said.

The wiki world is also spreading beyond the borders of Wales' many projects. Palo Alto–based Socialtext has turned wiki technology into a business tool for some 200 corporate customers such as Eastman Kodak Co.

"We're changing the way people work," said co-founder Ross Mayfield. "It's fostering a culture of working more collaboratively, sharing control of a common resource and fostering trust between them."

WikiHow, a how-to site founded by high-tech entrepreneurs Josh Hannah of Oakland and Jack Herrick of Palo Alto, emerged from the dotcom rubble. The two buddies purchased eHow, a dotcom that had seen better days, for an undisclosed sum early last year. Inspired by Wikipedia, they added a nonprofit wiki component to it at the beginning of this year.

"You want people who know, who are experts on how to do something, to write your articles," Hannah said.

Since then, the wiki portion has recorded 2.3 million hits, and some 1,200 contributors have added or edited how-to articles on topics such as how to "deal with impossible people" (advice: "do not make impossible people angry") and how to "find a gift for a self-proclaimed nerd or geek" ("Example cool gifts for a physics/math nerd would include: a super-egg, a snail-ball, orbitz soda, a home-brew holography kit, fog zero-blaster and a glass klein bottle.")

In each case, the wikis share the same basic foundation: If there's a mistake, you can immediately go in and fix it. If you disagree, or believe a topic needs further exploration, you can "fork" the article and start a new one.

And if nothing has been written on the subject you love, you can compose an article from scratch, using the site's template.

The site keeps a history of all edits, good and bad, enabling an article to revert back to an old version if necessary. A community of devotees act as administrators or janitors; they keep a close eye on changes and serve as clean-up crew. Try to sneak in something nasty about President Bush—a common occurrence on Wikipedia; earlier this week, someone replaced his biography with pictures of male genitalia—and a member of that community will remove it. (In the president's case, within minutes.) In extreme circumstances, the pages can be temporarily frozen to discourage vandalism.

In many cases, the authors and readers are one and the same: Bruce Yamamoto of Oakland consulted WikiHow for suggestions on organizing his monthly poker tournaments. He later turned around and authored an article on how to quickly calculate your odds in a poker game.

Ryan Holliday uses Wikitravel to look for off-the-beaten-path bars, restaurants and hang out spots in the Bay Area and Los Angeles. A frequent traveler who has trekked through Antarctica and the Galapagos Islands, he's also written articles on far-flung places that many tour books gloss over.

"When I first joined, I just dumped everything I knew (into Wikitravel) and other people finessed it," said Holliday, a 30-year-old web developer from Lafayette.

The idea is that, in the end, each change helps the information become more accurate, fair and full.

But it's not a perfect science. In a *USA Today* editorial, John Seigenthaler Sr., former assistant to Attorney General Robert Kennedy, detailed how someone had maliciously and incorrectly profiled him in a Wikipedia entry as a suspect in the Kennedy assassinations. He called the experience "Internet character assassination."

On Wikitravel, users have fought over the description of Israel and the occupation of the Gaza Strip. The bitter political debate over Taiwan and its relationship with China has also surfaced as users edit entries on Wikitravel.

"Our concern is about the traveler, not the politics," said Jensen, a Wikitravel contributor and administrator. "What really matters is what the traveler needs to know."

Critics have also questioned the trustworthiness of wikis. In an oft-quoted article, referenced even in Wikipedia's own explanation of itself, former *Encyclopedia Britannica* editor-in-chief Robert McHenry compared Wikipedia to using a public restroom: "It may be obviously dirty, so that he knows to exercise great care, or it may seem fairly clean, so that he may be lulled into a false sense of security. What he certainly does not know is who has used the facilities before him."

Consider e-mail as an analogy, said Hal Varian, a UC Berkeley information management professor. Early on, it became a useful tool for communication, allowing people to send messages to each other almost instantaneously. But it became less helpful as users were deluged with junk mail. The same could happen with wikis.

"It's possible it could be a victim of its own success. As more people chime in, you get a cacophony," said Varian, who nevertheless added that he finds Wikipedia a valuable resource.

> *"[The wiki] could be a victim of its own success. As more people chime in, you get a cacophony."*
> —Hal Varian, a professor at UC Berkeley

The *Los Angeles Times* experimented with a wiki a few months ago, posting an editorial on Iraq and opening it up for readers to edit. But the site was quickly overrun with "inappropriate material," namely pornographic messages and images, and within days the newspaper took down the site.

Another test by *Esquire* magazine offered better results. Editor-at-large A. Jacobs published a Wikipedia article on the Wikipedia site and opened the floor for editing. He wove in deliberate errors, including a claim that Wales has plans to create a "Wiki-constitution, a Wiki-Bible and Wiki-poetry." After 576 edits in three days, all but one of the mistakes were corrected.

"The one problem was it was a little pro-Wikipedia; there was a little hint of a press release to it," said Jacobs. "It wasn't quite as balanced as we would have done if we had written it ourselves. (But) overall they did a pretty good job. The writing was really good. . . . I was impressed and threatened. I was worried about my job."

Wales, the co-founder of Wikipedia, said the *Los Angeles Times* ran into trouble for two main reasons: it had not fostered an online community beforehand and it picked one of the most contentious issues around, Iraq. In comparison, the *Esquire* article took advantage of Wikipedia's well-established network and was largely a fact-based article.

"The software is not magic," Wales said. "You can't throw up a wiki and hope a miracle will occur. It takes thoughtful people to make it run."

Mayfield, the co-founder of Socialtext, added the information in wikis represents more of a "social truth. A wiki page represents the voice of a group on a topic. The quality is going to get better with the next edit."

Yamamoto, part of the WikiHow community, is helping build the site by penning new articles and fixing old ones.

"I was thinking about writing an article on how to procrastinate on WikiHow," Yamamoto said. "It's funny. The only reason to post that article is to procrastinate."

To Internet Stores, It's All About the Personal Touch

BY BOB TEDESCHI
THE NEW YORK TIMES, AUGUST 8, 2005

They are Internet upstarts, but they say they can take on Wal-Mart Stores, the world's biggest company.

The reason, they contend, is that they can offer you T-shirts with the design you want—your face on the back, say, paired with a cartoon on the front—that the giant retailer, for all of its $285.22 billion in revenue last year, simply can't match.

In other words, it's all about customization.

"In the offline world, there is a lot of consolidation in what people see and buy—the whole Wal-Mart, Clear Channel effect," said Fred Durham, the chief executive of CafePress.com, a six-year-old privately held company in the San Francisco Bay Area that acts as a marketplace for Internet sellers of tailor-made products like T-shirts and coffee mugs. "Online, there's more and more choice, and our tastes are getting more personalized, narrowly cast and focused."

Another online company that is going down same path as CafePress.com is Zazzle, a two-year-old manufacturer and retailer of personalized shirts, posters, greeting cards and postage. Meanwhile, more established Internet retailers like RedEnvelope and Lands' End, a division of Sears, are pushing forward with customization initiatives of their own.

Two developments help explain the trend. First, most Internet users now have access to high-speed connections, so it has become much easier for them to browse around for obscure items. And second, most Internet shoppers have bought books, CD's or airline tickets online and have acquired the confidence to attempt potentially more complicated purchases like clothes or custom gifts.

CafePress.com manufactures and ships customized goods for small online businesses affiliated with the site, which at the latest count numbered more than two million. Say you advertise silk shirts imprinted with a design of the customer's choosing. CafePress.com will make the product in one of its two plants and ship it within 24 hours. It will charge you $12 for the service; your profit is whatever you charge above that.

The company also sells music CD's and, beginning last month, customized stamps through a partnership with the online postage service Stamps.com. In all, it estimates, online consumers can choose from more than eight million designs—logos, slogans, cartoons, photos and the like—to emblazon on shirts, mugs, posters and mousepads. You can't find that kind of variety in a Wal-Mart store, it contends.

Wal-Mart doesn't appear to be taking the threat too seriously. Asked about it, Jacquie Young, a Wal-Mart spokeswoman, said: "Including Walmart.com, we offer dual convenience for customers, and above and beyond the assortment, to complement what we already have in the stores."

CafePress.com won't disclose revenues except to say that they are growing. It does say that it has 200 employees and has swung into the red after four consecutive years of profitability, despite raising $14 million early this year from a prominent venture capital firm. But that doesn't bother Mr. Durham. "We're spending dad's money a little bit, so we're not grossly unprofitable now, and we don't anticipate staying there for long," he said.

Like CafePress.com, Zazzle is privately held and located in the Bay Area. And like CafePress.com, it has received an infusion of venture capital funding—$16 million last month from some high-profile Silicon Valley investors—and says sales are growing. Zazzle has been profitable since its debut in 2003, according to Robert Beaver, its chief executive. And contrary to rhetoric about how customization can kill profit margins, margins at Zazzle "are very good," he said.

"We're a large-volume producer, so we've got strong buying power with our vendors," Mr. Beaver said. "And labor isn't as big a component in our manufacturing process as you might expect." He says company editors review orders for appropriateness and potential trademark infringements, then send them via the Web to a manufacturing plant in Menlo Park, Calif.

Customized shirts are both the most popular and the most labor-intensive product on the site, Mr. Beaver said. For each, employees must pull the proper shirt style from the shelves, move it to the printer and inspect the final product before it ships, all within 24 hours of the customer's order.

While Mr. Beaver acknowledged the close similarity between his company and CafePress.com, he pointed out that Zazzle allowed customers to combine and change many of the images offered, while CafePress.com customers print the images as they are displayed on the site.

Notable exceptions to Zazzle's customization policy are Coca-Cola, the Walt Disney Company and Fox's "Family Guy" series, which offer trademarked images for use on Zazzle. They, Mr. Beaver said, are more interested in marketing their brands.

One risk that start-ups in any field face is becoming so successful so fast that they can't keep up with orders, and online marketers are no exception. RedEnvelope, the online and catalog gift company, suffered a setback in the 2003 holiday season when it tried to sell too many personally embroidered and inscribed gifts before it was ready. Since then, RedEnvelope's chief executive, Alison L. May, has invested in new technology, equipment and labor to alleviate the problem.

For instance, Ms. May said, customers' orders for engraving or embroidery, which used to be typed out by employees, are now sent directly from RedEnvelope's servers to engraving and embroidery machines, speeding production and reducing errors. Other improvements, like organizing the personalized products into more logical batches, resulted in significant efficiency gains in recent months, Ms. May said.

RedEnvelope can use those gains as it seeks to reach profitability. Last week, the company announced that it had a loss of $1.75 million in the most recent fiscal quarter, compared with a loss of $950,000 in the same period last year. But revenues also increased, by 18 percent, to $25 million in the quarter.

And Lands' End has been busy upgrading its already substantial customization operation, which began with customized chinos in late 2001 and expanded to include custom jeans and dress shirts. Ed Whitehead, chief marketing officer for Lands' End, said the company was working on a system that eliminated the need for customers to type in a list of measurements and choose from a range of body types before determining the proper fit. The new system, which the company is currently testing, will allow users to "read your body type within 10 seconds," he said, "so we can move to market even more quickly."

Authorities Look to Net Predators

By Jill King Greenwood
Pittsburgh Tribune Review, October 9, 2005

With his fingers flying over the keyboard, Dennis Guzy assumes the identity of an 11-year-old girl.

He enters a chat room popular with preteen girls. He waits.

There are plenty of fish.

Within seconds, he's contacted by someone who starts the conversation benignly enough, then quickly redirects the online back-and-forth to a sexual nature.

Guzy is asked if he's ever had sex. He's asked to describe certain body parts. He's solicited for sex.

The conversation, from hello to sexual proposition, takes just minutes.

"We don't have to wait long," said Guzy, who heads the state attorney general's child predator unit. "Almost instantly, someone is contacting us, and right away they're discussing sex in very graphic terms. It happens every day."

The agents hope that by convincing a predator that he is talking to a child, they will build a case against that predator and keep him from victimizing a real child in the future.

"These guys are looking to steal the innocence of a child, and it's our job to keep that from happening," Guzy said.

Once a predator suggests a face-to-face meeting, the investigation kicks into high gear.

"We've had cases that have only lasted three hours from start to finish and others that have taken months," Guzy said. "We had a guy that contacted us, got very sexual, asked to meet us in person and within two hours was at the meeting spot."

In at least seven recent cases, that meeting spot has been a McDonald's restaurant in North Huntingdon, Westmoreland County. That's where agents arrested Thomas Rose on Sept. 16.

Authorities say Rose, the sports editor for the *Washington Observer-Reporter*, was corresponding a week earlier with "lilsweetchik12pa"—who identified herself as a 12-year-old girl named Jessica. He was really chatting with Lisa Ceh, one of three special agents with the child predator unit.

Rose, 52, of North Franklin, Washington County, was charged with criminal attempt, unlawful contact with a minor and criminal use of a communication facility to commit a crime. He is awaiting trial.

Guzy spends as many hours online as some teens, trolling chat rooms and Web sites and making himself a target for predators. He surfs the Web at all hours, on weekends and holidays.

They monitor chat rooms to see what real kids are discussing and to master their language and lingo.

It's not work for the faint of heart, Guzy said.

"Happens All the Time"

Law-enforcement officials nationwide arrest more than 6,000 Internet predators a year.

The Attorney General's office alone has arrested 80 men in the past three years—24 of them last year—for soliciting children for sex over the Internet and arranging in-person meetings for the

---

"Our children are posting too much personal information online, or they're responding to adults reaching out to them sexually online."—Parry Aftab, executive director of wiredsafety.org

---

purposes of sex, said Nils Hagen-Frederiksen, a spokesman for the Attorney General's Office. The conviction rate to date is 100 percent, he said.

The chance of a child being contacted online by someone soliciting sex is high, said Parry Aftab, executive director of the education and advocacy nonprofit wiredsafety.org, based in New York City.

Of children ages 13–16, one in four girls and one in seven boys will willingly meet someone off-line after meeting them online.

One in five kids ages 10 to 17 has received unwanted sexual solicitations online. The average age a child is first exposed to Internet pornography is 11.

"Anywhere, any place, any time, our children are posting too much personal information online, or they're responding to adults reaching out to them sexually online," Aftab said. "We see this in every type of child, from every type of background. . . . It happens all the time."

Aftab said children using the Internet tend to believe they're anonymous, and therefore don't think twice about posting personal information such as their real names, ages, the neighborhoods in which they live and the schools they attend. Many post photos of themselves and friends, Aftab said.

A Watchful Eye

Internet safety is a chief concern for Suzanne McWilliams of Mt. Lebanon, who has three daughters, ages 14, 16 and 18.

She has talked to her girls about how to use the Internet safely. She's installed software to block unsolicited advertisements and e-mails, and she monitors her daughters' Internet use.

She has some rules that are not negotiable.

"They cannot go into chat rooms, and they can't post profiles online with pictures and personal information that everyone can read," McWilliams said. "That is just so dangerous."

When her daughters were younger, the family had one computer in the living room. As they grew older, the girls earned their own computers, which are kept in their bedrooms, McWilliams said.

But McWilliams is still watching.

"Kids get too much a feeling of safety because the Internet is anonymous, and there's no one there looking over their shoulder," she said. "So I make sure I'm the one looking over their shoulder."

Tom Walker, co-president of the Fox Chapel Area High School Parent, Teacher, Student Association, said he's concerned about how easy it is for someone to reach a child online.

He has talked to his 16-year-old daughter Kathryn, used blocking software and told her to stay away from chat rooms.

But in the end, he said, you have to trust your child and hope that you've given him or her the tools to make responsible decisions.

"It really concerns me, but the reality is that kids today are growing up in a society where the Internet is a necessity," Walker said. "You can lock up your home computer, but they have computers in libraries and coffee houses, too. You just have to talk to your kids and trust them."

An Obsession

Often, Guzy said, the men he arrests have said they know law-enforcement officers are poaching for them and recognize they risk capture. But they can't seem to help themselves, Guzy said.

"During online conversations, they'll say to us, 'I hope you're not the police,'" Guzy said. "But they solicit us anyway and show up for an in-person meeting because they have an overwhelming urge to have sex with children. They throw caution away, and they're willing to take the risk. They just can't seem to help themselves. It's an obsession."

Al Danna, a special agent with Florida's Crimes Against Children Task Force, has lectured law-enforcement officers and prosecutors across the country about sexual predators.

Danna agreed with Guzy that many of the men he has investigated can't seem to resist the temptation.

"They have such an intense sexual drive that even when they know it's wrong, even when they know they're on probation or they could go to jail or they could be chatting with a cop and not a young girl, all logic flies out the window, and they do it anyway," said Danna, who has investigated child sex crimes for 25 years.

The best way for parents to keep their kids safe is to be aware of their online activities and to talk with them, Aftab said.

"Unless parents are going to monitor every piece of new technology we put in our kids' hands we have to rely on the filter between their ears—their brains—and their good judgment," Aftab said.

Guzy said he has asked the men he has arrested what advice they would give parents.

"They always say, 'If you don't love your children, I will,'" Guzy said.

How to Minimize Your Child's Risk:

- Don't set up a child's computer in the bedroom.
- Be aware of Web sites your children visit.
- Be suspicious if a child switches Web sites or turns off the computer when you walk into the room.
- Be aware of any suspicious phone calls, gifts or letters your child receives.
- Explain to your children that the Internet is an anonymous forum and they won't know who they're really communicating with.
- Encourage your kids to talk to you about what they see online and to report any unwanted solicitations.
- Purchase blocking software.
- Tell children never to give out their names, addresses, phone numbers or other personal information.
- Tell you children never to agree to meet in person someone they've met online.

SOURCE: Pennsylvania Attorney General's office and www.wiredsafety.org

Internet Predators by the Numbers:

- Of children ages 13–16, one in four girls and one in seven boys will meet someone from a chat room in person.
- Most kids victimized by Internet predators are between the ages of 11½ and 15.
- Of all victims, 70 percent are girls.
- Law-enforcement officials each year arrest more than 6,000 Internet predators.
- One in five kids ages 10 to 17 have received unwanted sexual solicitations online.
- The average age a child is first exposed to pornography on the Internet is 11.
- An estimated 100,000 Web sites contain child pornography.

SOURCE: Pennsylvania Attorney General's office and the U.S. Justice Department's Youth Internet Safety Survey

Caught in a Spiral of Gaming

By Victor Gonzales
The Seattle Times, July 6, 2005

Nothing was more absorbing to Jared Osborne than online gaming.

The allure of friends around the world and the seemingly perfect world gaming offered were keeping him online 18 to 20 hours a day for weeks on end.

Responsibilities would beckon, but he'd keep promising himself "just another 10 minutes playing online everything from 'Anarchy Online' to 'City of Heroes' to 'Counter-Strike'"—"literally every single multiplayer online game out there."

Meanwhile, his real-life problems went unsolved, his homework went undone and he was screwing up jobs at Arby's and Jack In The Box.

All this caused him anxiety, and he coped by telling himself his procrastination freed time for gaming.

"And oddly enough, you get a relief," he said. ". . . The more you do it, the easier it gets."

Osborne, 24, of Kenmore, now knows that he was clinically addicted to online gaming. He is not alone.

As the Internet and technology weave into everyday life, some mental-health professionals say Internet Addiction Disorders are ever more common.

So many have fallen into the thrall of electronic gaming that in April a specialty practice opened in Redmond.

Mental-health counselors Hilarie Cash and Kim McDaniel started Reality Quest, a clinical program for electronic-gaming addiction with eight counselors and an intervention specialist. It's a spinoff of and shares offices with Internet/Computer Addiction Services (I/CAS), which was launched in 1998.

Conflicting Views

When a person becomes dependent on the euphoria he experiences playing video games, he is addicted, said Cash.

"They're preoccupied with gaming; they get irritable when they are not gaming. They play compulsively—that is, they play even though they know its hurts" their emotions and health.

The stereotypical gaming addict is a male teenager with low self-esteem, but anyone with money to buy a computer system can become addicted, Cash said. People going through an emotional time, or who are lonely, bored or shy, may be particularly vulnerable.

One of Cash's first gaming-addiction cases was in 1994: a normal, successful, married man working for Microsoft. Before he recovered, the man's addiction cost him his marriage and his job. In another case, a teenager pulled a knife when his father tried to take away the computer, she said.

> *The prevalence and seriousness of Internet addictions remain the subject of debate.*

Yet the prevalence and seriousness of Internet addictions remain the subject of debate. Dr. Joseph McGlinchey, a postdoctoral fellow in psychiatry at Brown University, says the issue gets more attention than it deserves.

As a graduate student at the University of Washington, he did his dissertation on Internet addiction, focusing on college students, a group he thought most likely to have excessive Internet use.

"The rate of those who had major problems with using the Internet—like thinking their use was out of control, or failing classes because of it—was overall very low," he said.

Dr. Donn Marshall, chief psychologist of counseling at the University of Puget Sound, disagrees that concern is overblown and sees Internet addiction leading to other problems, such as depression.

What makes the Internet so potent, he said, is the variety of and easy access to stimuli.

"If gaming is your vulnerability, games are available via the Net 24/7," he said. "If you are drawn to anonymous sex or pornography, it is at your virtual disposal at the click of a mouse. If you are a compulsive shopper, this store never closes."

Getting out of the Game

Getting gaming addicts to log off is a long process and not always successful, Cash said. She figures about 50 percent of those she treats recover.

The therapy is often particularly difficult because many people need computers and the Internet in their jobs, Marshall said.

Cash's methods vary from one-hour personal sessions to two-hour therapy groups that include family members. For children and teens, McDaniel suggests family therapy coupled with participation in community-service projects and team sports to reinforce the sessions.

The length of treatment varies, but is typically between two and eight months. Cost varies by case. Cash says insurance may cover treatment, and cost concessions are sometimes made.

Whatever shape it takes, the aim of therapy is always the same: to teach addicted gamers how to set limits on computer use and to help them develop the social and stress-management skills to overcome their addictions, Cash said.

Ironically, there are self-help forums, Web logs and Web sites designed to help people overcome video-game and Internet addiction, but Cash isn't a fan.

"Going online for help is like conducting an [Alcoholics Anonymous] meeting in a bar," she said. It might be a start, she said, but nothing can replace personal interaction.

Osborne started seeing Cash last year. His dad made addiction treatment a condition for Osborne to live at home.

Today, Osborne says he needed an uninvolved third party such as Cash to listen as he vented his frustrations and problems. The therapy gave him the opportunity to scrutinize his life. His parents' concern was warranted, he said, "but it was hard to see without 20/20 hindsight."

Offline Problems

Osborne started playing video games at age 4. Eventually, he used them to cope with real-life problems: depression, painful conflicts with friends and a high-school environment that didn't challenge him. At 18, he had what he calls a nervous breakdown that lasted three months.

"I was absolutely incoherent. . . . I literally did nothing. I just stared at the wall. I didn't care if I lived or died."

He slowly recovered and later graduated from high school.

For the next six years, Osborne moved often, staying with friends and family, unable to cope with his lingering depression and lack of motivation. After he moved in with his dad in February 2004, his gaming increased dramatically.

As his problems and community college grades worsened, he pursued other distractions, like reading, but the bulk of his time was spent online.

"It was escapism," he said. "But instead of getting away from my problems, it put me right into the thick of it."

An offline introvert, Osborne was an online extrovert, creating friendships in multiplayer games that were as meaningful and real as those away from the computer. He felt comfortable talking to people from around the world, baring himself through the keyboard. He even met some online people in real life.

The games were utterly absorbing and offered a measure of control he didn't have offline.

"You will not run into unexpected situations in games," he said. "There's a set of rules that you know the game will not break. You choose to fight your battles on your grounds and on your terms."

In contrast, "Life picks the battles for you. Life does not have to make sense," he said.

"Sticky Factors"

All video games, but multiplayer online games in particular, have features that keep gamers coming back, said Wendy Kays, a consultant to Reality Quest.

Opinions differ on specifics, but the primary traits, called "sticky factors," are the increasing difficulty levels, the increasing amount of time and teamwork required to play, and the involved relationships that develop with other players, she said.

Another enticement, McDaniel said, is the "God effect."

"You can step into a world and decide who lives and who dies and what to create and what to destroy," she said. It represents a semblance of control in life.

That small measure of control, she said, is used to cope with the pressures of life, friends, school and growing up.

It took years before Osborne started to realize that he was going nowhere. He paid for those years with his health (at 5-foot-10, he weighs 287 pounds), poor grades, dead-end jobs, the threat of homelessness and the loss of his family's respect.

Finally, "I began to clue in," he said. "And I realized . . . I just need to do it."

Still Logging On

Osborne still plays online games, though he has internal controls—"mental slappings," he calls them—to keep from playing for days on end. Regaining the respect of his family is an uphill battle, he admits. He's started a job as a electronic technician's apprentice and has begun bicycling and walking to get into shape.

Does he regret his time online?

"I've made friendships online," he said. "And I've made close friends with people from all around the world. . . . But . . . I've done practically nothing else with my life. I've accomplished nothing. There is no résumé for gaming."

Information on the Web

Reality Quest Institute: http://www.realityquestinstitute.org/

The Center for Online and Internet Addiction: http://netaddiction.com/

American Academy of Pediatrics' Opinion on Media Use: http://www.aap.org/healthtopics/mediause.cfm

Online Gamers Anonymous: http://www.olganon.org/index.htm

Internet Addiction Guide: http://psychcentral.com/netaddiction/

Are You Addicted?

If the answer is yes to five or more questions below, you may be addicted to being online or electronic gaming:

Are you unable to predict the amount of time you will spend online or gaming?

Do you have attempts to control the behavior for an extended period of time?

Do you have a sense of euphoria while engaged in the activity?

Are you craving more time online or gaming?

Are you neglecting family and friends?

Are you feeling restless, irritable or discontent when not engaged in the activity?

Are you lying to family and employers about the habit?

Are you experiencing problems with school or job performance?

Are you feeling guilt, shame, anxiety or depression as a result of the behavior?

Do you have changing sleep patterns?

Are you developing health issues such as carpal tunnel syndrome, eye strain, weight change and backaches?

Are you denying, rationalizing, and minimizing adverse consequences stemming from use?

Are you withdrawing from real-life hobbies and social interactions?

Do you obsess about sexual acting out through gaming or other Internet applications?

Do you have an enhanced persona to find cyberlove or cybersex?

Source: Reality Quest Institute Web site

Appendix

Is It O.K. to Be a Luddite?

By Thomas Pynchon
The New York Times Book Review, October 28, 1984

As if being 1984 weren't enough, it's also the 25th anniversary this year of C. P. Snow's famous Rede lecture, "The Two Cultures and the Scientific Revolution," notable for its warning that intellectual life in the West was becoming increasingly polarized into "literary" and "scientific" factions, each doomed not to understand or appreciate the other. The lecture was originally meant to address such matters as curriculum reform in the age of Sputnik and the role of technology in the development of what would soon be known as the third world. But it was the two-culture formulation that got people's attention. In fact it kicked up an amazing row in its day. To some already simplified points, further reductions were made, provoking certain remarks, name-calling, even intemperate rejoinders, giving the whole affair, though attenuated by the mists of time, a distinctly cranky look.

Today nobody could get away with making such a distinction. Since 1959, we have come to live among flows of data more vast than anything the world has seen. Demystification is the order of our day, all the cats are jumping out of all the bags and even beginning to mingle. We immediately suspect ego insecurity in people who may still try to hide behind the jargon of a specialty or pretend to some data base forever "beyond" the reach of a layman. Anybody with the time, literacy and access fee these days can get together with just about any piece of specialized knowledge s/he may need. So, to that extent, the two-cultures quarrel can no longer be sustained. As a visit to any local library or magazine rack will easily confirm, there are now so many more than two cultures that the problem has really become how to find the time to read anything outside one's own specialty.

What has persisted, after a long quarter century, is the element of human character. C. P. Snow, with the reflexes of a novelist after all, sought to identify not only two kinds of education but also two kinds of personality. Fragmentary echoes of old disputes, of unforgotten offense taken in the course of long-ago high-table chitchat, may have helped form the subtext for Snow's immoderate, and thus celebrated, assertion, "If we forget the scientific culture, then the rest of intellectuals have never tried, wanted, or been able to understand the Industrial Revolution." Such "intellectuals," for the most part "literary," were supposed, by Lord Snow, to be "natural Luddites."

Except maybe for Brainy Smurf, it's hard to imagine anybody these days wanting to be called a literary intellectual, though it doesn't sound so bad if you broaden the labeling to, say, "people who read and think." Being called a Luddite is another matter. It brings up questions such as, Is there something about reading and thinking that would cause or predispose a person to turn Luddite? Is it O.K. to be a Luddite? And come to think of it, what is a Luddite, anyway?

Historically, Luddites flourished in Britain from about 1811 to 1816. They were bands of men, organized, masked, anonymous, whose object was to destroy machinery used mostly in the textile industry. They swore allegiance not to any British king but to their own King Ludd. It isn't clear whether they called themselves Luddites, although they were so termed by both friends and enemies. C. P. Snow's use of the word was clearly polemical, wishing to imply an irrational fear and hatred of science and technology. Luddites had, in this view, come to be imagined as the counter-revolutionaries of that "Industrial Revolution" which their modern versions have "never tried, wanted, or been able to understand."

But the Industrial Revolution was not, like the American and French Revolutions of about the same period, a violent struggle with a beginning, middle and end. It was smoother, less conclusive, more like an accelerated passage in a long evolution. The phrase was first popularized a hundred years ago by the historian Arnold Toynbee, and has had its share of revisionist attention, lately in the July 1984 *Scientific American*. Here, in "Medieval Roots of the Industrial Revolution," Terry S. Reynolds suggests that the early role of the steam engine (1765) may have been overdramatized. Far from being revolutionary, much of the machinery that steam was coming to drive had already long been in place, having in fact been driven by water power since the Middle Ages. Nevertheless, the idea of a technosocial "revolution," in which the same people came out on top as in France and America, has proven of use to many over the years, not least to those who, like C. P. Snow, have thought that in "Luddite" they have discovered a way to call those with whom they disagree both politically reactionary and anti-capitalist at the same time.

But the *Oxford English Dictionary* has an interesting tale to tell. In 1779, in a village somewhere in Leicestershire, one Ned Lud broke into a house and "in a fit of insane rage" destroyed two machines used for knitting hosiery. Word got around. Soon, whenever a stocking-frame was found sabotaged—this had been going on, sez the *Encyclopedia Britannica*, since about 1710—folks would respond with the catch phrase "Lud must have been here." By the time his name was taken up by the frame-breakers of 1812, historical Ned Lud was well absorbed into the more or less sarcastic nickname "King (or Captain) Ludd," and was now all mystery, resonance and dark fun: a more-than-human presence, out in the night, roaming the hosiery districts of England, possessed by a single comic shtick—every time he spots a stocking-frame he goes crazy and proceeds to trash it.

But it's important to remember that the target even of the original assault of 1779, like many machines of the Industrial Revolution, was not a new piece of technology. The stocking-frame had been around since 1589, when, according to the folklore, it was invented by the Rev. William Lee, out of pure meanness. Seems that Lee was in love with a young woman who was more interested in her knitting than in him. He'd show up at her place. "Sorry, Rev, got some knitting." "What, again?" After a while, unable to deal with this kind of rejection, Lee, not, like Ned Lud, in any fit of insane rage, but let's imagine logically and coolly, vowed to invent a machine that would make the hand-knitting of hosiery obsolete. And he did. According to the encyclopedia, the jilted cleric's frame "was so perfect in its conception that it continued to be the only mechanical means of knitting for hundreds of years."

Now, given that kind of time span, it's just not easy to think of Ned Lud as a technophobic crazy. No doubt what people admired and mythologized him for was the vigor and single-mindedness of his assault. But the words "fit of insane rage" are third-hand and at least 68 years after the event. And Ned Lud's anger was not directed at the machines, not exactly. I like to think of it more as the controlled, martial-arts type anger of the dedicated Badass.

There is a long folk history of this figure, the Badass. He is usually male, and while sometimes earning the quizzical tolerance of women, is almost universally admired by men for two basic virtues: he is Bad, and he is Big. Bad meaning not morally evil, necessarily, more like able to work mischief on a large scale. What is important here is the amplifying of scale, the multiplication of effect.

The knitting machines which provoked the first Luddite disturbances had been putting people out of work for well over two centuries. Everybody saw this happening—it became part of daily life. They also saw the machines coming more and more to be the property of men who did not work, only owned and hired. It took no German philosopher, then or later, to point out what this did, had been doing, to wages and jobs. Public feeling about the machines could never have been simple unreasoning horror, but likely something more complex: the love/hate that grows up between humans and machinery—especially when it's been around for a while—not to mention serious resentment toward at least two multiplications of effect that were seen as unfair and threatening. One was the concentration of capital that each machine represented, and the other was the ability of each machine to put a certain number of humans out of work—to be "worth" that many human souls. What gave King Ludd his special Bad charisma, took him from local hero to nationwide public enemy, was that he went up against these amplified, multiplied, more than human opponents and prevailed. When times are hard, and we feel at the mercy of forces many times more powerful, don't we, in seeking some equalizer, turn, if only in imagination, in wish, to the Badass—the djinn, the golem, the hulk, the superhero—who will resist what otherwise would overwhelm us? Of course, the real or secular frame-bashing was still being done by everyday folks, trade unionists ahead of their time, using the night, and their own solidarity and discipline, to achieve their multiplications of effect.

It was open-eyed class war. The movement had its Parliamentary allies, among them Lord Byron, whose maiden speech in the House of Lords in 1812 compassionately argued against a bill proposing, among other repressive measures, to make frame-breaking punishable by death. "Are you not near the Luddites?" he wrote from Venice to Thomas Moore. "By the Lord! if there's a row, but I'll be among ye! How go on the weavers—the breakers of frames— the Lutherans of politics—the reformers?" He includes an "amiable chanson," which proves to be a Luddite hymn so inflammatory that it wasn't published till after the poet's death. The letter is dated December 1816: Byron had spent the summer previous in Switzerland, cooped up for a while in the Villa Diodati with the Shelleys, watching the rain come down, while they all told each other ghost stories. By that December, as it happened, Mary Shelley was working on Chapter Four of her novel *Frankenstein, or the Modern Prometheus*.

If there were such a genre as the Luddite novel, this one, warning of what can happen when technology, and those who practice it, get out of hand, would be the first and among the best. Victor Frankenstein's creature also, surely, qualifies as a major literary Badass. "I resolved . . . ," Victor tells us, "to make the being of a gigantic stature, that is to say, about eight feet in height, and proportionally large," which takes care of Big. The story of how he got to be so Bad is the heart of the novel, sheltered innermost: told to Victor in the first person by the creature himself, then nested inside of Victor's own narrative, which is nested in its turn in the letters of the arctic explorer Robert Walton. However much of *Frankenstein*'s longevity is owing to the undersung genius James Whale, who translated it to film, it remains today more than well worth reading, for all the reasons we read novels, as well as for the much more limited question of its Luddite value: that is, for its attempt, through literary means which are nocturnal and deal in disguise, to *deny the machine*.

Look, for example, at Victor's account of how he assembles and animates his creature. He must, of course, be a little vague about the details, but we're left with a procedure that seems to include surgery, electricity (though nothing like Whale's galvanic extravaganzas), chemistry, even, from dark hints about Paracelsus and Albertus Magnus, the still recently discredited form of magic known as alchemy. What is clear, though, despite the commonly depicted Bolt Through the Neck, is that neither the method nor the creature that results is mechanical.

This is one of several interesting similarities between *Frankenstein* and an earlier tale of the Bad and Big, *The Castle of Otranto* (1765), by Horace Walpole, usually regarded as the first Gothic novel. For one thing, both authors, in presenting their books to the public, used voices not their own. Mary Shelley's preface was written by her husband, Percy, who was pretending to be her. Not till 15 years later did she write an introduction to *Frankenstein* in her own voice. Walpole, on the other hand, gave his book an entire made-up publishing history, claiming it was a translation from medieval Italian. Only in his preface to the second edition did he admit authorship.

The novels are also of strikingly similar nocturnal origin: both resulted from episodes of lucid dreaming. Mary Shelley, that ghost-story summer in Geneva, trying to get to sleep one midnight, suddenly beheld the creature being brought to life, the images arising in her mind "with a vividness far beyond the usual bounds of reverie." Walpole had been awakened from a dream, "of which, all I could remember was, that I had thought myself in an ancient castle . . . and that on the uppermost bannister of a great stair-case I saw a gigantic hand in armour."

In Walpole's novel, this hand shows up as the hand of Alfonso the Good, former Prince of Otranto and, despite his epithet, the castle's resident Badass. Alfonso, like Frankenstein's creature, is assembled from pieces—sable-plumed helmet, foot, leg, sword, all of them, like the hand, quite oversized—which fall from the sky or just materialize here and there about the castle grounds, relentless as Freud's slow return of the repressed. The activating agencies, again like those in *Frankenstein*, are non-mechanical. The final assembly of "the form of Alfonso, dilated to an immense magnitude," is achieved through supernatural means: a family curse, and the intercession of Otranto's patron saint.

The craze for Gothic fiction after *The Castle of Otranto* was grounded, I suspect, in deep and religious yearnings for that earlier mythical time which had come to be known as the Age of Miracles. In ways more and less literal, folks in the 18th century believed that once upon a time all kinds of things had been possible which were no longer so. Giants, dragons, spells. The laws of nature had not been so strictly formulated back then. What had once been true working magic had, by the Age of Reason, degenerated into mere machinery. Blake's dark Satanic mills represented an old magic that, like Satan, had fallen from grace. As religion was being more and more secularized into Deism and nonbelief, the abiding human hunger for evidence of God and afterlife, for salvation—bodily resurrection, if possible—remained. The Methodist movement and the American Great Awakening were only two sectors on a broad front of resistance to the Age of Reason, a front which included Radicalism and Freemasonry as well as Luddites and the Gothic novel. Each in its way expressed the same profound unwillingness to give up elements of faith, however "irrational," to an emerging technopolitical order that might or might not know what it was doing. "Gothic" became code for "medieval," and that has remained code for "miraculous," on through Pre-Raphaelites, turn-of-the-century tarot cards, space opera in the pulps and comics, down to *Star Wars* and contemporary tales of sword and sorcery.

To insist on the miraculous is to deny to the machine at least some of its claims on us, to assert the limited wish that living things, earthly and otherwise, may on occasion become Bad and Big enough to take part in transcendent doings. By this theory, for example, *King Kong* (?-1933) becomes your classic Luddite saint. The final dialogue in the movie, you recall, goes: "Well, the airplanes got him." "No . . . it was Beauty killed the Beast." In which again we encounter the same Snovian Disjunction, only different, between the human and the technological.

But if we do insist upon fictional violations of the laws of nature—of space, time, thermodynamics, and the big one, mortality itself—then we risk being judged by the literary mainstream as Insufficiently Serious. Being serious about these matters is one way that adults have traditionally defined themselves against the confidently immortal children they must deal with. Looking back on *Frankenstein*, which she wrote when she was 19, Mary Shelley said, "I have an affection for it, for it was the offspring of happy days, when death and grief were but words which found no true echo in my heart." The Gothic attitude in general, because it used images of death and ghostly survival toward no more responsible end than special effects and cheap thrills, was judged not Serious enough and confined to its own part of town. It is not the only neighborhood in the great City of Literature so, let us say, closely defined. In westerns, the good people always win. In romance novels, love conquers all. In whodunits, murder, being a pretext for a logical puzzle, is hardly ever an irrational act. In science fiction, where entire worlds may be generated from simple sets of axioms, the constraints of our own everyday world are routinely transcended. In each of these cases we know better. We say, "But the world isn't like that." These genres, by insisting on what is contrary to fact, fail to be Serious enough, and so they get redlined under the label "escapist fare."

This is especially unfortunate in the case of science fiction, in which the decade after Hiroshima saw one of the most remarkable flowerings of literary talent and, quite often, genius, in our history. It was just as important as the Beat movement going on at the same time, certainly more important than mainstream fiction, which with only a few exceptions had been paralyzed by the political climate of the cold war and McCarthy years. Besides being a nearly ideal synthesis of the Two Cultures, science fiction also happens to have been one of the principal refuges, in our time, for those of Luddite persuasion.

By 1945, the factory system—which, more than any piece of machinery, was the real and major result of the Industrial Revolution—had been extended to include the Manhattan Project, the German long-range rocket program and the death camps, such as Auschwitz. It has taken no major gift of prophecy to see how these three curves of development might plausibly converge, and before too long. Since Hiroshima, we have watched nuclear weapons multiply out of control, and delivery systems acquire, for global purposes, unlimited range and accuracy. An unblinking acceptance of a holocaust running to seven- and eight-figure body counts has become—among those who, particularly since 1980, have been guiding our military policies—conventional wisdom.

To people who were writing science fiction in the 50's, none of this was much of a surprise, though modern Luddite imaginations have yet to come up with any countercritter Bad and Big enough, even in the most irresponsible of fictions, to begin to compare with what would happen in a nuclear war. So, in the science fiction of the Atomic Age and the cold war, we see the Luddite impulse to deny the machine taking a different direction. The hardware angle got de-emphasized in favor of more humanistic concerns—exotic cultural evolutions and social scenarios, paradoxes and games with space/time, wild philosophical questions—most of it sharing, as the critical literature has amply discussed, a definition of "human" as particularly distinguished from "machine." Like their earlier counterparts, 20th-century Luddites looked back yearningly to another age—curiously, the same Age of Reason which had forced the first Luddites into nostalgia for the Age of Miracles.

But we now live, we are told, in the Computer Age. What is the outlook for Luddite sensibility? Will mainframes attract the same hostile attention as knitting frames once did? I really doubt it. Writers of all descriptions are stampeding to buy word processors. Machines have already become so user-friendly that even the most unreconstructed of Luddites can be charmed into laying down the old sledgehammer and stroking a few keys instead. Beyond this seems to be a growing consensus that knowledge really is power, that there is a pretty straightforward conversion between money and information, and that somehow, if the logistics can be worked out, miracles may yet be possible. If this is so, Luddites may at last have come to stand on common ground with their Snovian adversaries, the cheerful army of technocrats who were supposed to have the "future in their bones." It may be only a new form of the perennial Luddite ambivalence about machines, or it may be that the deepest Luddite hope of miracle has now come to reside in the computer's ability to get the right data to those whom the data will do the most good. With the proper deployment of budget and computer time, we will cure cancer, save ourselves from nuclear extinction, grow food for everybody, detoxify the results of industrial greed gone berserk—realize all the wistful pipe dreams of our days.

The word "Luddite" continues to be applied with contempt to anyone with doubts about technology, especially the nuclear kind. Luddites today are no longer faced with human factory owners and vulnerable machines. As well-known President and unintentional Luddite D. D. Eisenhower prophesied when he left office, there is now a permanent power establishment of admirals, generals and corporate CEO's, up against whom us average poor bastards are completely outclassed, although Ike didn't put it quite that way. We are all supposed to keep tranquil and allow it to go on, even though, because of the data revolution, it becomes every day less possible to fool any of the people any of the time.

If our world survives, the next great challenge to watch out for will come— you heard it here first—when the curves of research and development in artificial intelligence, molecular biology and robotics all converge. Oboy. It will be amazing and unpredictable, and even the biggest of brass, let us devoutly hope, are going to be caught flat-footed. It is certainly something for all good Luddites to look forward to if, God willing, we should live so long. Meantime, as Americans, we can take comfort, however minimal and cold, from Lord Byron's mischievously improvised song, in which he, like other observers of the time, saw clear identification between the first Luddites and our own revolutionary origins. It begins:

As the Liberty lads o'er the sea
Bought their freedom, and cheaply, with blood,
So we, boys, we
Will die fighting, or live free,
And down with all kings but King Ludd!

Bibliography

Books

Alavi, Nasrin. *We Are Iran: The Persian Blogs*. New York: Soft Skull Press, 2005.

Anderson, Brian C. *South Park Conservatives: The Revolt Against Liberal Media Bias*. Washington, D.C.: Regnery Publishing, 2005.

Bagdikian, Ben H. *The New Media Monopoly*. Boston: Beacon Press, 2004.

Bakardjieva, Maria. *Internet Society: The Internet in Everyday Life*. London: Sage Publications Inc., 2005.

Calavita, Marco. *Apprehending Politics: News Media and Individual Political Development*. Albany: State University of New York, 2005.

Cooke, Miriam, and Bruce B. Lawrence. *Muslim Networks from Hajj to Hip Hop*. Chapel Hill: University of North Carolina Press, 2005.

Davis, Richard. *Politics Online: Blogs, Chatrooms, and Discussion Groups in American Democracy*. New York: Routledge, 2005.

Davis, Richard, and Diana Owen. *New Media and American Politics*. Oxford, U.K.: Oxford University Press, 2004.

Dibona, Chris, et al. *Open Sources 2.0*. Sebastopol, Calif.: O'Reilly Media, 2005.

Eickelman, Dale F., and Jon W. Anderson, eds. *New Media in the Muslim World*. Bloomington: Indiana University Press, 1999.

Farkas, Bart G. *Secrets of Podcasting, Second Edition: Audio Blogging for the Masses*. Berkeley: Peachpit Press, 2006.

Fenton, Tom. *Bad News: The Decline of Reporting, the Business of News, and the Danger to Us All*. New York: Regan Books, 2005.

Flew, Terry. *New Media: An Introduction*. New York: Oxford University Press, 2005.

Gillmor, Dan. *We the Media*. Sebastopol, Calif.: O'Reilly Media, 2004.

Harris, Dan, ed. *The New Media Book*. London: British Film Institute, 2002.

Hewitt, Hugh. *Blog: Understanding the Information Reformation That's Changing Your World*. Nashville: Nelson Business, 2005.

Hirsen, James. *Hollywood Nation: Left Coast Lies, Old Media Spin, and New Media Revolution*. Three Rivers, Mich.: Three Rivers Press, 2006.

Howley, Kevin. *Community Media: People, Places, and Communication Technologies*. Cambridge: Cambridge University Press, 2005.

Jones, Steve. *Encyclopedia of New Media: An Essential Reference to Communication and Technology*. London: Sage Publications Inc., 2003.

Khuns, Peter, et al. *Blogosphere: Best of Blogs*. Indianapolis: Que, 2006.

Kline, David, et al. *Blog: How the Newest Media Revolution Is Changing Politics, Business, and Culture*. New York: CDS Books, 2005.

Lister, Martin, ed. *New Media: A Critical Introduction*. London and New York: Routledge, 2003.

Louw, Eric. *The Media and Political Process*. London: Sage Publications, 2005.

Manovich, Lev. *The Language of New Media*. Cambridge, Mass.: The MIT Press, 2001.

McChesney, Robert, et al. *The Future of Media: Resistance and Reform in the 21st Century*. New York: Seven Stories Press, 2005.

McClary, Maclyn. *Issues in Journalism: A Discussion Guide for News Media Ethics*. North Charleston, S.C.: Book Surge Publishing, 2005.

McLuhan, Marshall. *The Medium Is the Message*. Corte Madera, Calif.: Gingko Press, 2005 [1967].

O'Brien, Barbara. *Blogging America: Political Discourse in a Digital Nation*. Wilsonville, Ore.: William James & Company, 2004.

Rushkoff, Douglas. *Cyberia: Life in the Trenches of Cyberspace*. Manchester, U.K.: Clinamen Press Ltd., 2002.

Ryan, Marie-Laure. *Narrative Across Media: The Languages of Storytelling*. Lincoln: University of Nebraska Press, 2004.

Sakr, Naomi, ed. *Women and Media in the Middle East. Power Through Self-Expression*. London: I.B. Tauris, 2004.

Stauffer, Tom. *Blog On: Building Online Communities with Web Logs*. Columbus, Oh.: Osborne/McGraw-Hill, 2002.

Straubhaar, Joseph, and Robert Larose. *Media Now: Understanding Media, Culture, and Technology (with CD-ROM and Infotrac)*. Belmont, Calif.: Thomson Wadsworth, 2006.

Viguerie, Richard A., and David Franke. *America's Right Turn: How Conservatives Used New and Alternative Media to Take Over America*. Chicago: Bonus Books, 2004.

Young, David. *Why We Blog*. Austin: Wizard Academy Press, 2004.

Web Sites

Readers seeking additional information about the new media may wish to refer to the following Web sites, all of which were operational as of this writing.

Digital Deliverance

www.digitaldeliverance.com/philosophy/definition/definition.html

At this site is an essay on media, using the term in its original sense (that is, as the plural form of the word *medium*) and rejecting the meaning the word has acquired in recent years (that is, the communications industry). In the online and print versions of his newspaper, the essay's author argues that the rise of the Internet has resulted in a new medium of communication that essentially differs from the media available in the past.

Douglas Rushkoff

www.rushkoff.com

Douglas Rushkoff, a major commentator on the new-media revolution, provides links to interviews, articles (both old and new), and a downloadable PDF file of a version of his book *Open Source Democracy*.

The Journal of New Media and Culture

www.ibiblio.org/nmediac

This site contains links to volumes of the journal dating back to 2002, containing both essays about the new media and audiovisual pieces exploring the culture of the Internet, its environment, ideologies, and the experiences of those using the technology.

MasterNewMedia

www.masternewmedia.org

This regularly updated Web site provides links to a variety of articles on new Internet technologies, industry developments, and the most popular news, research, and blogs on the Internet.

Media, Culture and Meaning

www.colorado.edu/journalism/mcm/index.htm

Media, Culture and Meaning is a site run by the University of Colorado's Center for Mass Media, the stated goal of which is to explore the relationship between today's mass media and old-fashioned storytelling.

New Media Musings

www.newmediamusings.com

This site, run by J. D. Lasica, the new-media authority and author of *Darknet: Hollywood's War Against the Digital Generation* (2005), is primarily a blog (a few years old) that keeps its readers abreast of new-media developments and provides links to other Web sites of interest.

Poems That Go

www.poemsthatgo.com/ideas.htm

This is an Internet journal that publishes both literary artworks and essays about how the new media is changing the literary aesthetics. It also contains a moderated discussion among the readers—that is, readers may submit comments about the journal or the works published in it to a public forum, but an editor must approve those comments before they are posted.

Rebuilding Media

rebuildingmedia.corante.com

Formatted like a blog, this regularly updated site contains articles about the media written by Vin Crosbie, Dorian Benkoil, Bob Cauthorn, and Ben Compaine, all of whom have a background in print journalism but have since embraced the new media. There is also a link to Corante.com, the site hosting Rebuilding Media, which contains other blogs of interest.

Resource Center for Cyberculture Studies

www.com.washington.edu/rccs/

This Web site is the home of an online organization that was formed to create a collaborative learning environment "to research, teach, support, and create diverse and dynamic elements of cyberculture." The site provides essays, book reviews, links to relevant sites, and more.

Additional Periodical Articles with Abstracts

More information about the new media and related subjects can be found in the following articles. Readers who require a more comprehensive selection are advised to consult the *Readers' Guide Abstracts*, *Social Sciences Abstracts*, and other H.W. Wilson Publications.

Bright Future for Newspapers. Paul A. Farhi. *American Journalism Review*, v. 27 pp54–59 June/July 2005.

Newspapers are in a good position to thrive in the new-media age, Farhi reports. Although circulation numbers have been on a downward trajectory for two decades and the Internet appears set to make newspapers redundant, media stories about the rise and fall of newspapers are greatly exaggerated. Newspapers are doing no worse, and in some cases better, than other elements of the media, including the Internet. Young people do not read newspapers, but they are not interested in news from any source, and this is a problem for news organizations of all types, including those on the Internet. Newspapers also enjoy some unique competitive advantages, and in a world of ever-expanding choice, many people, pressed for time and seeking the trusted and familiar, may stick with what they already know and respect. It will take skill, vision, and creativity for newspapers to survive, Farhi concludes, but survival is a far more likely outcome than failure.

Hold That Obit. Rem Rieder. *American Journalism Review*, v. 27 p6 April/May 2005.

The battered mainstream media are down but not out, Rieder argues. The nascent blogosphere has played a critical role in two recent episodes. The blogging community eviscerated CBS's massively flawed report on President Bush's National Guard Service. It also gave more attention than did the mainstream media to off-the-record assertions by CNN honcho Eason Jordan that U.S. troops had targeted journalists in Iraq. CNN failed to recognize that the controversy was not going to go away and, perhaps in an overreaction, Jordan stepped down. The much-maligned mainstream media have to cover the news, and it is difficult to imagine anyone else carrying out this costly, labor-intensive business, Rieder concludes, and even though the media landscape has changed dramatically in recent years, no economic model has emerged to finance a full-scale news-gathering operation in cyberspace.

Republican Rout. Michael Barone. *The American Spectator*, v. 37 pp10–14 December 2004/January 2005.

President George W. Bush's reelection has two important ramifications, Barone writes. First, it establishes, or goes a long way toward establishing, the GOP as the majority party in the United States. Indeed, the fact that Bush won in less than perfect circumstances, with a war raging and economic recovery not certain, reveals the strength of the Republican Party. Second, Bush's success administered a knockout blow to the credibility and position of old media in U.S. society, which dominated news coverage of past presidential races but was this year challenged and, for many voters, replaced by new media—talk radio, Fox News, and the bloggers. What is more, during this campaign, Barone concludes, old media overreached itself in its frantic and increasingly transparent desire to crush Bush.

Voices of the People. Stephen Baker. *Business Week*, pp78–80 September 26, 2005.

In this piece, part of a special section on the best of the Web for socializing, sharing, and creating, Baker reports that audience participation is giving new Web sites their spark. The public provides all of the content on PostSecret, now the tenth most-popular blog site of the 13 million monitored by the blog search engine Feedster.com. Every day, hundreds of people illustrate and caption their confessions on postcards and send them to an address in Germantown, Maryland, where art and pop-culture fan Frank Warren chooses the best and posts them on PostSecret. New music sites such as Pandora allow users to hear tracks by their favorite artists, share their mixes by sending them in e-mails to friends, or purchase songs by forwarding users to iTunes or Amazon.com.

The New Radio Revolution. Heather Green, et al. *Business Week*, p325 March 14, 2005.

The writers anticipate that the competition for profits in the exploding radio-programming industry will be ferocious. The digitalization of the industry means barriers to entry are less and less important, opening up the field to a host of new players, including satellite-radio start-ups XM and Sirius, new-media behemoths Yahoo! and MSN, as well as ordinary individuals. Traditional radio players are already feeling the impact, with Viacom Inc. announcing a $10.9 billion write-down in assets at its Infinity Broadcasting Corp. division and the nation's biggest radio chain, Clear Channel Communications Inc., taking a $4.9 billion write-down on its radio licenses. New technology means more people than ever will be producing and listening to audio programming.

From Exiles to Empire Builders? Ronald Grover. *Business Week*, pp40–41 April 4, 2005.

Moguls in exile are currently the hottest act in show business, Grover reports. After years of masterminding relentless consolidation, a small but growing group of former movers and shakers is now observing from the sidelines as media giants split up. In the wake of Viacom Inc.'s recent breakup announcement, the new media buzzword is deconsolidation, and the best people to preside over new media combinations built out of the old are often the individuals who originally assembled these large companies and are now on the outside with the knowledge of how they work and the means to get them back, according to former Universal Studios CEO Frank J. Biondi Jr. Indeed, industry heavyweights, such as former Viacom Entertainment Group CEO Jonathan L. Dolgen, former AOL Time Warner COO Robert W. Pittman, and former Telecommunications Inc. president Leo J. Hindery Jr., are all putting up money for deals.

Distance Learning: An Academic Leader's Perspective on a Disruptive Product. Lloyd Armstrong. *Change*, v. 32 pp20–27 November/December 2000.

Armstrong believes that the Internet and other new-media technologies have the potential to convert distance learning (DL) into a force that could transform the face of higher education. One of the vital steps in such an exercise is to anticipate the possible effects of Internet-Mediated DL (IMDL) and other new media on one's own educational markets and internal organization. IMDL delivers several new benefits not seen in traditional classroom teaching, including convenience, scalability, global access, and lower cost structure. On the other hand, Armstrong notes, by eliminating restrictions on the number of students who can be taught by a top institution or a star professor at any one time, IMDL has the potential to exacerbate massively the winner-take-all tendencies of higher education, thus becoming a very disruptive product for all but the top-ranking institutions.

Saving Journalism. Philip Meyer. *Columbia Journalism Review*, v. 43 pp55–57 November/December 2004.

Meyer proposes that journalism is being phased out by increasing levels of advertising, press agentry, and entertainment, and the only way to save it is to develop a new model that finds profit in truth, vigilance, and social responsibility. If journalism and its social-service functions are to be preserved, it may be best to look for ways to keep the spirit and tradition of socially responsible journalism alive until it finds a home in some new media form whose nature is not yet known. One way to preserve journalism's standards while waiting for a new business model to be born is for the profession to reconsider its chronic reluctance to regulate itself, as other professions do, on both moral and technical grounds.

State of the Art: Their War. Daniel Schulman. *Columbia Journalism Review*, v. 44 p13 September/October 2005.

Soldiers are using Internet blogs to reveal their experiences on the front lines, Schulman reports. Most media coverage of the war in Iraq does not portray the ordinary U.S. soldier in a personal way, but readers who want a taste of the soldier's life can access "milblogs," which have been appearing in increasing numbers since the start of the war in March 2003. Some of these are sophomoric and obscenity-filled, whereas others provide frank and poignant accounts of the reality of the situation in Iraq. The blogs have attracted the interest of book publishers as well as military leaders, who are concerned that they could breach operational security. The Pentagon is also worried that blogging soldiers could affect how the flow of information from the field is managed.

Blogworld and Its Gravity Personal. Matt Welch. *Columbia Journalism Review*, v. 42 pp21–26 September/October 2003.

In this piece, part of a special section on the new age of alternative media, Welch contends that a new breed of amateur journalist is emerging via weblogs and doing some interesting things. In a manner reminiscent of old-style metro columnists or the liveliest of the New Journalists, many of these writers are developing strong ties to their readers, while others are defining the narrowest of editorial territories as their own—for example, appellate court rulings, new media proliferation in Tehran, and the meeting of hip-hop and libertarianism. These individuals bring four qualities to journalism: personality, eyewitness testimony, editorial filtering, and uncounted gigabytes of new knowledge. Moreover, Welch notes, blogs are a great cheap development system for talent because there are tens of thousands of potential columnists writing for free and working in a free market where the best rises to the top rapidly.

Culture in the Age of Blogging. Terry Teachout. *Commentary*, v. 119 pp39–48 June 2005.

Recent surveys carried out by the Pew Internet & American Life Project have revealed that 11 million American adults claim to have started weblogs, or blogs, and that 27 percent of Internet users say that they read these Internet-based journals, Teachout reports. These blogs are part of a technology-driven, new-media revolution. Until recently, the mainstream media had a monopoly on presenting the news to substantial numbers of Americans. This started to change in the late 1990s, however, when the earliest blogs appeared on the Internet. Today, Americans are increasingly embracing the new Web-based media, which present a proliferating variety of outlooks and styles of communication. The writer reflects on the ways that blogs are transforming American culture, and he discusses his own blog, "About Last Night: Terry Teachout on the Arts in New York City."

This Is Your Brain on Clicks. Lea Goldman. *Forbes*, v. 175 p54 May 9, 2005.

In Beijing, the Communist Youth League reportedly held a weeklong camp in April for about a dozen children who were addicted to the Internet, Goldman writes. The problem is so widespread—approximately 15 percent of Chinese teenagers are said to suffer from "Internet addiction disorder"—that Shanghai elementary school pupils are now given lectures on broadband burnout as well as the usual antidrug warnings. This condition is not mentioned in either the World Health Organization's International Classification of Diseases or in the

American Psychiatric Association's handbook, the *Diagnostic and Statistical Manual of Mental Disorder*s, but such experts as Maressa Hecht Orzack, director of the Computer Addiction Study Center at Harvard's McLean Hospital, claim that between 5 and 10 percent of Web surfers experience Web dependency. They suffer cravings and withdrawal symptoms in much the same way as a frustrated compulsive gambler.

The 75-Year-Old Killer App. Geoffrey Colvin. *Fortune*, v. 146 p76 October 14, 2002.

All that people throughout the world will do with more bandwidth is watch television, Colvin states. The explosion of bandwidth availability has the entire technology industry sensing that some mind-bending new application will be next to gain dominance. In the United States, as in the world in general, however, people are devouring as much television as is made available by technology. The explosion in bandwidth available anywhere anytime and on any device is wonderful, but what people actually want is more television. Maybe the key to success in the new media world is not technology leadership, radically new business models, or innovative services; maybe, Colvin suggests, it is programming.

Invasion of the Podcast People. Peter Lewis. *Fortune*, v. 152 pp204+ July 25, 2005.

Podcasters are transforming radio by creating their own audio broadcasts with PCs, microphones, and portable MP3 players, Lewis reports. There are an estimated 6,000 to 7,000 regular podcasters at present, offering audio programs on the Web for fun and perhaps someday for fame and profit. Locating and listening to podcasts recently became a lot easier with the release of Apple's iTunes 4.9, a free download from apple.com. This new version of iTunes permits users of Windows or Mac OS X computers to look for podcasts by keyword, subscribe to them for automatic updates, and transfer them to an iPod, allowing them to be played at the listener's place and time of convenience. The writer provides advice on creating a podcast.

Games, Cookies, and the Future of Education. Henry Kelly. *Issues in Science and Technology*, v. 21 pp33–40 Summer 2005.

Advanced information technologies should be properly exploited to improve American education, according to Kelly. There is now almost universal agreement that something should be done about education standards in the U.S., which lag behind those of other industrialized countries. Although holding students and school systems to high standards is necessary to remedy the problem, there is also a need to better understand how students learn and to design and implement new tools to take advantage of this understanding. Spectacular developments in computer processor power, mobile devices, and the software required to deliver entertainment, answer consumer questions, and run simulations for science and engineering have the potential to reshape learning, but an adequately funded, well-managed program of federal research, and demonstration in learning science and technology is needed to take full advantage of these tools.

How Computers Make Our Kids Stupid. Sue Ferguson. *Maclean's*, v. 118 pp24–30 June 6, 2005.

There is increasing evidence that computers can have a negative effect on children's education, Ferguson notes. Although they can be engaging and useful tools for learning, computers and the Internet can also distract children from homework, promote superficial and uncritical thinking, replace face-to-face interaction between students and teachers, and prompt compulsive behavior. Perhaps the most convincing evidence for taking a more critical view of computers is a broad, rigorous study published in November 2004 by University of Munich economists Thomas Fuchs and Ludger Woessmann. Fuchs and Woessmann examined the results of the OECD's PISA international standardized tests, and their results indicated that the sheer ubiquity of information technology is impeding learning: Once household income and the wealth of a school's resources are extracted from the equation, teenagers with the most access to computers and the Internet at home and school produce the worst test scores.

"I'm Engaged in Online Foreplay." Danylo Hawaleshka. *Maclean's*, v. 118 pp 60–61 September 19, 2005.

Generally viewed as a safe online community, Habbo Hotel has developed into a powerful global player for teen money and attention, becoming one of the Internet's most popular nonviolent sites for teenagers, Hawaleshka reports. Worldwide, Habbo attracts 4 million unique browser visits every month, according to Internet monitor Nielsen/NetRatings, and Sulake Corp., Habbo's Helsinki-based parent company, claims that revenue totaled $20 million in 2004. The first Habbo Hotel was established in Britain in 2001, and there are now sites in 16 countries, including Canada, Australia, Japan, and Spain. According to Det. Staff Sgt. Arni Stinnissen, who works in the Ontario Provincial Police's electronic crimes section, the Canadian Habbo operation uses a number of excellent safety features, including a protocol for informing law enforcement if, for example, a predator is present.

Media Feast. Jason Snell. *Macworld*, v. 22 p7 October 2005.

The writer outlines the features of Podcasts and the Core Pocket Media Player, which offer users more freedom of choice in media consumption.

A Loser's Game. Reuven Frank. *The New Leader*, v. 88 pp42–4 September/ October 2005.

In the last few years, many have debated the conventional wisdom that each new media technology overwhelms its predecessor; according to Frank, this debate received its most prominent—and perhaps most magisterial—expression in a recent article in the *New York Times Book Review* by Richard A. Posner. In the essay, Posner suggested that newspapers will soon die out, that the success of Fox's right-wing cable news channel has forced CNN and others to move to the left, and that the news is less accurate. Posner and others are partly correct, and it is inarguable that the audience for news in all media is shrinking or that technological change affects the medium favored by those seeking news, Frank concedes, but these are actually separate issues and not a new phenomenon.

Google's Book Battle. Brad Stone. *Newsweek*, v. 146 p50 October 31, 2005.

Five major publishers, acting through the Association of American Publishers, are suing Google over its plan to put whole libraries online, Stone reports. The publishers contend that by creating electronic copies of books, the search giant is committing massive copyright infringement. The suit could merely become a footnote in the dramatic tale of Google's growth—it recently announced a 700 percent jump in quarterly earnings over 2004—but it could also portend dark times ahead. Google's aggressive schemes for expansion include making copies of videos, photos, and news articles to add to its powerful search index. The book publishers, among others, argue that these plans encroach on their rights. Ultimately, Stone concludes, the outcome of the case will depend on the legal interpretation of fair use, which takes into account whether copying is for commercial or noncommercial use, and whether it damages the potential market of the copyrighted work.

Premodern America. Kurt Andersen. *New York*, v. 38 pp32+ March 14–21, 2005.

Journalism is reverting to the status quo of the mid-19th century, when most coverage was partisan, Andersen argues. At that time, New York City had over a dozen dailies and countless weeklies, most of which were small-scale and idiosyncratic reflections of their editors and owners, full of summaries of stories lifted from other publications. It took the next 100 years for the U.S. press to fully adopt the idea of a journalism that aspires to an impartial, empirical rigor that transcends party and ideology. Over the last two decades, new technologies have enabled a profitable rendition of journalism, such as blogging, that allows for the return of overt partisanship and quirks of sensibility.

In Tiny Arab State, Web Takes on Ruling Elite. Neil MacFarquhar. *The New York Times*, p1+ January 15, 2006.

Ali Abdulemann is Bahrain's most notorious blogger, MacFarquhar observes, in this piece, part of a series entitled "Stirrings in the Deseart," about political change in the Middle East. In a nation where the royal family possessess unparalleled influence, holding half the cabinet positions and the major posts in the security service and the University of Bahrain, Mr. Abdulemann uses the Internet to criticize the ruling elites and call for democracy. His site is a prime example of the power of the Internet to foment discontent.

Easy Listening. Rob Walker. *The New York Times Magazine*, p20 January 23, 2005.

The California-based public radio station KCRW.com is trying to create an alliance between new and old media by building an online listener base and, in the process, seeking to develop what amounts to a national brand, Walker reports. For the past few years, KCRW.com has broadcast three "streams," including a 24-hour music option. Stations such as KCRW have become crucial to idiosyncratic bands and the smaller record labels that promote them, as well as to the music consumers who want to be surprised.

Podcasts, Explained. Adam Wasserman. *Opera News*, v. 70 pp58–59 December 2005.

Wasserman provides an operagoer's guide to "podcasts," or music delivered in MP3 format. He explains the technology, how to procure a podcast, and the enticement podcasting offers to the average operagoer. He also considers the availability of opera-specific podcasts, which, though scant right now, is likely to increase in the future since the demand certainly exists.

DIY: Create Your Own Podcasts. Larry Magid. *PC Magazine*, v. 24 pp66–67 October 18, 2005.

Podcasting allows individuals to create their own programming, Magid observes. This programming can be listened to on an iPod, another portable music player, or a PC—all that is required is a microphone, a PC, some free or low-cost software, and an Internet connection. Magid also provides instructions for creating a podcast.

Why Google Print Is More Important than You Think. Michael J. Miller. *PC Magazine*, v. 24 pp7–8 December 27, 2005.

Google's plan to scan and digitize thousands of books and make them searchable online may be laudable, but there are some caveats, Miller notes. Google is launching its Print Library Project with the aim of making more of the world's knowledge accessible to more people, but it again raises the question of how the rights of those who created the content should be treated. Google claims it will feature books that are covered by copyright, unless the copyright holders specifically refuse to cooperate, but representatives of the authors and publishers have filed suit to prevent Google from featuring any copyrighted books unless the copyright holder has agreed to opt in, prompting Google to start scanning only out-of-print books in November. If a court decides that Google must get the book-copyright holders' permission, a ruling may come down eventually stipulating that Google index only Web sites for which it has the publishers' permission—thus ruining the whole concept of Web search as it is currently understood.

Media on Your Time. Chad Denton. *Smart Computing*, v. 16 p17 June 2005.

Technology is making it easier than ever to control audio entertainment, Denton observes. Podcasting is one new way of wielding greater control over personal audio. The launch of portable video players and the fact that some amateur producers are already starting to toy with video mean that the podcast will probably yield to the vidcast but, given that podcasting can be done while biking, running, or driving, portable video may make less sense. Denton also outlines his approach to podcasting.

Blogging 2.0. Jeremy Caplan. *Time*, v. 166 p86 September 26, 2005.

Caplan offers advice on the best Web sites with which to navigate the blogosphere, how to set up a blog, and the top five blogs as determined by the number of Web sites linking to them.

Messengers of Cool. Jeremy Caplan. *Time*, v. 166 p98 October 24, 2005.

In this article, part of a special section on the world of the future, Caplan explores the concept of "cool hunting," or the monitoring of urban trends. Though cool hunting stretches back more than 10 years, new digital networks are transforming the rules of the game. During the last three years, the widespread use of blogs, podcasts, Web sites, and newsletters has taken cool hunting away from the control of professional marketers, moving it to the text-message-happy fingers of amateur trend trackers. Some independent Internet sites are primarily concerned with broad trends and generational changes in consumer habits, but others concentrate on styles, foods, brands, and gadgets that have found favor among trendsetters.

Yahoo! Goes Hollywood. Terry McCarthy. *Time*, v. 165 pp50–52 March 21, 2005.

Former movie chief Terry Semel believes that Yahoo! can lure the entertainment industry to the Internet, McCarthy reports. Although Internet companies have long wanted to put entertainment content online, concerns about piracy, illegal downloading, and disruption of their revenue model have caused the studios to maintain a tight grip on their product. Semel, who spent 30 years in Hollywood before being brought in to run Yahoo!, is determined to change things. In November 2004, he appointed former ABC Entertainment chairman Lloyd Braun to run a new media division in Los Angeles. Moreover, Yahoo!'s recent deal with Mark Burnett, which gave the company exclusive Internet rights to the second season of *The Apprentice,* was groundbreaking. Semel is now hoping that his company's presence in Los Angeles will enable it to get the deals when they begin to flow.

The Wild, Wild Web. Mortimer B. Zuckerman. *U.S. News & World Report*, v. 139 p76 December 5, 2005.

According to Zuckerman, a new age of journalism is challenging the "trustee model" of journalism, in which journalistic professionals act as gatekeepers, filtering the defamatory and the false. At present, a large section of the public believes the new media is inflecting their reporting so as to tell people not so much how the world works but how the media believe it ought to work. While fragmenting the mass audience and containing more inaccuracies than mainstream media, blogs (weblogs) have democratized journalism by providing citizens with daily and immediate access to different opinions and occasionally to those with expert knowledge.

Indymedia. Lila Kitaeff. *Utne*, pp85–86 January/February 2003.

In this article, part of a special section on the Internet, Kitaeff reports that protesters with media capabilities, known as Indymedia, have emerged throughout the world, according to Anita Hayhoe of the University of Toronto's *Ryerson Review of Journalism*. Seattle witnessed the full potential of this new medium during the 1999 protests against the World Trade Organization. By then, activists had taken to the streets equipped with video cameras, cell phones, and laptops. Thanks to the Internet, their images of riot police shooting rubber bullets at protesters was seen worldwide, which directly contradicted statements by Seattle's chief of police, who denied on major network news shows that such methods had been employed. According to Kitaeff, the biggest challenge for the future of the independent media is providing alternative media to poor communities, where levels of computer literacy and availability are low.

The Blogs of War. John Hockenberry. *Wired*, v. 13 pp118–123+ August 2005.

The Pentagon is very concerned about blogs written by members of the American armed forces, Hockenberry observes. Military bloggers are refreshingly honest about the war in Iraq, and they express views that range from the far right to far left. A new policy introduced this spring obligates all military bloggers inside Iraq to register with their units, and it directs commanders to carry out quarterly reviews of blogs to ensure that bloggers are not divulging casualty information or infringing on operational security or privacy rules. Hockenberry also profiles a number of military bloggers.

File-Sharing Is, Like, Totally Uncool. Jeff Howe. *Wired*, v. 12 pp133+ May 2004.

A lesson plan called "What's the Diff?: A Guide to Digital Citizenship," sponsored and funded by the Motion Picture Association of America (MPAA), has reached just over half a million junior high students since it started this school year, Howe reports. The point of the program, according to MPAA spokesperson Rich Taylor, is for pupils to reach their own conclusions about being a good digital citizen. The true point, however, is to safeguard Hollywood from the fate of the record industry. The music business has already suffered from peer-to-peer file sharing, but the movie industry has thus far remained largely untouched. The writer discusses the different reactions to the program by students in California's San Fernando Valley and in a working-class neighborhood of Yonkers, New York.

Index